The No-Nonsense Guide to Mental Health in Schools

Responding to the rise in challenges to the mental health of young people, this book provides schoolteachers with the essential skills required to recognise emotional distress in their students and, more importantly, empowers them to make a genuine difference.

Teachers have unintentionally become the 'first responders' for distressed youth in their schools, but they cannot be expected to carry out mental health interventions. This book provides teachers with essential mental health literacy and knowledge of mental health first aid so that they know how to act when their students need help. The chapters provide concise and jargon-free outlines of the main mental disorders that teachers can expect to encounter in their classrooms and offer practical guidance on how to speak to these students and help them towards the most suitable support in the community. Drawing on the best available research and offering illustrative case studies to support core skills, this book gives teachers the confidence and competence to take action.

A crucial resource for all school staff, *The No-Nonsense Guide to Mental Health in Schools* supports teachers to feel confident in making a difference in the wellbeing of their students.

John R. Burns is a clinical psychologist based in Sydney, Australia. He has an extensive career history working as a clinician and researcher in the field of school mental health and has published articles, scientific papers and book chapters. He received his PhD from Macquarie University, where he now serves as an Adjunct Fellow in the School of Psychological Sciences.

"Dr Burns has masterfully combined the latest scientific evidence with his own immense clinical expertise to create an engaging and accessible guide for educators wanting to learn how to better support their students' mental health. In a series of ten brief and extremely readable chapters, he guides us through the essential steps from recognising when there may be a concern, to having discussions with students and parents, to connecting them with evidence-based support. This is a book with potential to make a real difference for schools, educators, families, and – most importantly – young people."

Emma Soneson PhD, *Department of Psychiatry, University of Oxford, UK*

"Dr. Burns discusses the role of educators in supporting student mental health in a down-to-earth, friendly style that will resonate with teachers. He draws the readers in with the stifling reality of youth mental health challenges, real-world examples, and a call to the compassion and humanity of educators. Burns' conversational style will engage readers as they learn about the nature and prevalence of mental health challenges and how they present in the classroom. He then offers concrete, reasonably implemented strategies for identifying and addressing student mental health concerns and creating safe, supportive environments. This is a must-read for any educator who wishes to foster the well-being of their students while also helping them achieve academically."

Sharon Hoover PhD, *Professor, Division of Child and Adolescent Psychiatry, Co-Director, National Center for School Mental Health, University of Maryland, USA*

"An indispensable and timely resource! Highly accessible to educators of all backgrounds, this book is a must-read for both seasoned and novice educators, and it deserves a place in training programs for educators and school staff. What truly sets it apart is the way it honours and respects teachers and students alike. The book ensures that teachers are up to date with the best knowledge and strategies available in the field, all while holding teacher expertise and student safety in the highest regard. With a wealth of experience in real school settings, the author offers invaluable insights and practical guidance that empower teachers to provide evidence-based support to children and young people within the school environment."

Professor Jennie Hudson, *Black Dog Institute, University of New South Wales, Sydney, Australia*

"Dr Burns brings a wealth of knowledge and experience to this body of work, constantly highlighting the value of teachers and those on the front line, in identifying, protecting, and guiding students through daily or micro-interactions. Armed with a wisdom borne of years working with young people and teachers, John's pragmatic, caring, and respectful approach provides a light to practitioners, as we help navigate the complexities of daily life for young people."

Dr Briony Scott, *Principal, Wenona, President, The Australian Council for Educational Leaders, Australia*

"Through his warm and conversational tone, Dr Burns has provided a very informed text grounded in vital research regarding what we need to know about some of our most vulnerable students. What we love about this book, is that Dr Burns has been able to communicate in easy-to-access and personable ways to busy educators, what they need to know quickly and well. It is very clear that Dr Burns cares about kids and about the wonderful educators who go to work every day to teach and support them."

Associate Professor Judith Howard and Dr Meegan Brown, *School of Early Childhood and Inclusive Education, Queensland University of Technology, Australia*

"If you're a teacher seeking information about how to help students in your classroom experiencing mental health disorders, this book is for you. For administrators, John's book is the resource you've been looking for to guide your professional development group. Each chapter grounded in research and evidence-based practices includes vignettes and practical strategies grounded in reality that 21st century educators are crying for. Throughout all this, John's message rings clear: this book is about saving students."

Associate Professor Richard E. Cleveland, *College of Education, Georgia Southern University, USA*

"A deeply informed and easy to read book for every teacher who wishes to become a well-equipped front-line worker in holding back the well-documented and disturbingly unyielding invasion of emotional distress in children and adolescents. This insightful book provides broad knowledge and deep understanding of mental health issues, how they impact students and classes, and how teachers can make a profound difference."

Associate Professor Anne Maj Nielsen, *Danish School of Education, Aarhus University, Denmark*

"*The No-Nonsense Guide to School Mental Health* is an extraordinary guide for new and experienced educators alike. Dr Burns' years of practical experience in schools provides a grounded perspective of the issues and a sense of purpose about the actions of teachers. The book is indeed a "call to action" but not to just any action. There is clear guidance for teachers, all of whom share the concern for student wellbeing and safety. We all have our part to play, and this book guides us through terrain we find hard to navigate. This book should be on the reading list for all teachers in their years of training or at some stage of their career."

Dr Peter Miller, *Principal, The Geelong College, Australia*

The No-Nonsense Guide to Mental Health in Schools

What Every Teacher Can Do to Make a Difference

John R. Burns, PhD

Foreword by
Ronald M. Rapee, PhD, AM, FASSA

LONDON AND NEW YORK

Designed cover image: © Getty Images

First published 2024
by Routledge
4 Park Square, Milton Park, Abingdon, Oxon OX14 4RN

and by Routledge
605 Third Avenue, New York, NY 10158

Routledge is an imprint of the Taylor & Francis Group, an informa business

© 2024 John R. Burns

The right of John R. Burns to be identified as author of this work has been asserted in accordance with sections 77 and 78 of the Copyright, Designs and Patents Act 1988.

All rights reserved. No part of this book may be reprinted or reproduced or utilised in any form or by any electronic, mechanical, or other means, now known or hereafter invented, including photocopying and recording, or in any information storage or retrieval system, without permission in writing from the publishers.

Trademark notice: Product or corporate names may be trademarks or registered trademarks, and are used only for identification and explanation without intent to infringe.

British Library Cataloguing-in-Publication Data
A catalogue record for this book is available from the British Library

ISBN: 978-1-032-43509-1 (hbk)
ISBN: 978-1-032-43508-4 (pbk)
ISBN: 978-1-003-36766-6 (ebk)

DOI: 10.4324/9781003367666

Typeset in Optima
by Apex CoVantage, LLC

Contents

Acknowledgements	viii
Foreword by Professor Ronald M. Rapee	ix
Introduction	**1**
1 The case for mental health in schools	7
2 How would I know if a student has a disorder?	20
3 Recognising internalising disorders	35
4 Recognising externalising disorders	50
5 Other disorders we can expect in schools	64
6 Raising concerns with students	81
7 Classroom approaches to students with emotional and behavioural disorders	97
8 Self-harming and suicidal students	117
9 Getting help	132
10 Self-care for school staff	153
Epilogue	177
Index	179

Acknowledgements

The ideas in this book are based on the teaching that I have received over many decades. I've been taught about mental health theory and practice by my lecturers across the universities where I have studied. I've been taught about the relentless desire to expand our knowledge of things that matter by my colleagues in the research community. I've been taught about the passion of shaping the lives of students by the outstanding educators I've worked alongside. But without doubt, I've been taught the most by the countless young people who have sat in my counselling office and, with honesty, vulnerability and courage, shared the realities of their lives, their fears, their hopes, their trials and their triumphs. My great thanks to each and every one of you.

Foreword

In thinking about how to introduce this book, two key moments from my recent professional life sprang to mind. The first was in 2009, when John Burns approached me to begin his PhD under my supervision. John had been working for many years as a school psychologist, and he had seen how many young people struggle with mental health issues that were undetected and unhelped. John expressed a passion to find these young people before it was too late and get them the help they needed. As he expressed it, he wanted to 'get them onto the radar'. Part of John's research involved developing a questionnaire that could help to identify young people who were at heightened risk for mental health problems, and he called this questionnaire the RADAR. John taught me that one way to proactively reduce mental health problems in young people was to ask them about their mental health, and he introduced me to a growing research field referred to as 'universal mental health screening'. Universal mental health screening is the principle of screening an entire population of young people (such as an entire grade group or entire school) and identifying those young people who are struggling with their mental health but have yet to get any help for it. At the time, this very logical approach was being increasingly tested in the United States but had not yet received much interest elsewhere.

The second key moment of relevance to this book came a few years later, in 2017, when I was approached by a dedicated educator, Ian Bowsher. At the time, Ian was the principal of Barrenjoey High, a secondary school on Sydney's Northern Beaches. Despite its idyllic location, Ian had noticed how many of the students appeared to be struggling with mental health issues, leading a couple to end up taking their own lives. Ian came to me to ask whether there was any way we could be more proactive about getting

Foreword

help to these young people earlier rather than waiting until it was too late. Following the impact that John had had on my thinking, I introduced Ian to the concept of universal mental health screening, and I happily volunteered to help him set this up at Barrenjoey High. Two years later, Ian's passion had spread, and we were screening students in 15 schools across Sydney's Northern Beaches.

As an addendum to these two stories, at the time of writing this foreword, my colleagues and I have been engaged by the Australian Department of Education to build a national system to screen students from all Australian schools, identify those who are currently struggling with issues related to mental health, and help to guide them and their families toward appropriate pathways to care. This voluntary mental health check tool, which we have called My Mind Check, will transform the ways in which schools are able to proactively help their students and will hopefully begin to reduce the burden of mental health in Australia. It has come about at least partly through the passion of people like John and Ian.

Mental health is one of the key issues facing youth today. In the second Australian Child and Adolescent Survey of Mental Health and Wellbeing (Young Minds Matter), one in seven (14%) young people aged 4 to 17 reported a clinically diagnosable mental disorder. Sadly, if repeated today, this figure would likely be even higher, since several reports indicate that mental health problems among young people are increasing. What is most alarming is that only half of these young people had received any help over the previous year, and there is evidence that even the half who are getting help are not getting the most appropriate or the best help. Clearly, we are not doing enough for our young people, and there are far too many who are struggling with their wellbeing on their own.

Earlier in my career, I remember being told very clearly that the purpose of schooling is to teach the 'three R's'. Gradually over the decades, that aim has broadened. In recent years, there has been increasing recognition that schools have a critical role to play in helping students with their mental health. At least in part, this recognition has grown from the understanding that mental health and education are vitally intertwined. The Young Minds Matter survey has shown very dramatically how much young people with mental health problems struggle academically. As I noted earlier, one key role that schools can play is to support regular mental health checks to identify young people who are struggling with mental health and support them into appropriate pathways to care. This might be thought of as a 'bottom up' approach – listening to the voices of students. However, another and often-overlooked way that schools can support student mental health is to upskill teachers in their knowledge about mental health. This is not to say that teachers need to become quasi-mental health professionals. Rather, simply by increasing their understanding and recognition of mental health difficulties, teachers are in the ideal position to support their students' mental health, to provide an empathetic and informed environment, and to appropriately talk with students who they suspect might be struggling and help them find appropriate external supports.

John's book is a natural extension of the work of this visionary man. In our changing society, *The No-Nonsense Guide to Mental Health in Schools* is now a must-read for all educators. It will help to upskill education staff in their knowledge and understanding of mental health in young people. By doing so, it plays a crucial role in the supportive context that our society needs if we are to reverse the trend toward increasing levels of mental health difficulties among our young people.

Ronald M. Rapee PhD, AM, FASSA
Distinguished Professor of Psychology
Macquarie University

# Introduction

Life-changing events are rare, but when they happen, your whole life gets knocked onto a different path. Sometimes, they start in seemingly innocuous ways; sometimes, they are random occurrences; sometimes, they are the results of the actions of others. Sometimes, they are for the better, sometimes for the worst, and sometimes, they just 'are'.

For me, it started with a phone message. I had been out that night, perhaps until 10 p.m. When I got home, I noticed the flashing light on my telephone answering machine. (It was 2009, and we still used landlines and home answering machines!) I was going to leave it until the morning, but my wife encouraged me to check it. It was the principal of my school. His message was brief: 'John, it's Tim here. We have a critical incident'. I called him straight back. A student in Year 9 at our school had taken his own life earlier that night. We had less than 10 hours to prepare for our critical incident response the next day. Needless to say, the days and weeks that followed were brutal for our school community.

It wasn't until some months later that I had the time and headspace to reflect on this event. This wasn't the first student death we had managed during my time at the school. It wasn't even the first suicide that we had navigated as a school team. But there was something about this death which now, more than a dozen years on, continues to profoundly disturb me at both a personal and professional level. And here's the kicker – *no one knew that this young man was suicidal*. His death was a total surprise to everyone. How can that happen? How can a boy who attended school every day, who saw six different class teachers every day, who met numerous times a week with a pastoral care teacher, who had a stack of good friends, who walked past a school psychologist's office (my office!) every day – *how could no one have picked up that he was distressed enough to end his own life?*

Introduction

It was this phone call, this news, and this question that has been a life-changing event for me. Since that day in 2009, working as a psychologist in a school ceased being a convenient job to pay the bills. Rather, it is now a passion, a 'vocation' and a life pursuit. Every day, my mind is occupied with the challenge of how we, staff in schools, can be better at identifying young people who need help and making sure they get it.

When I was a school student, I was lucky. I made friends easily enough, I was an OK student, I had a supportive family, and I enjoyed good physical and mental health. It's only now, since I've become a psychologist, that I reflect on the difficulties of my school-yard peers. I didn't think twice about Nick, the kid who I avoided and even excluded for six years but who I now can see had an autism spectrum disorder.[1] In Year 11, when most of my mates had developed strong interests in girls, cars and sport, Nick continued with his special interest in building (and constantly talking about) Lego. I don't think I was a ringleader in teasing Nick, but to my shame, I joined in the choir of kids calling out across the playground 'Hey Lego Boy'.

Or what about Jay, the boy who I can now see had Tourette's syndrome. Not knowing any better, kids in our year group – and indeed in those in the years above and below – used to mercilessly mimic his tics. I remember my admiration for Paul, the kid who got drunk and smoked drugs every weekend. At the time, I thought with envy that these were the signs of a cool and mature kid. Now, however, I believe them to be the signs of a desperately unhappy young man who had no better mechanisms to cope with whatever demons were going on for him behind the scenes. By chance, I ran into Paul a few years ago. He greeted me with a smile, and we got chatting. After a bit, I threw out the question, 'What have you been doing since school?' At that point, the smile melted away from his face as he explained that he had suffered with severe depression for many years, had never been able to hold down a job, and was now unemployed and had moved back to his parents' house.

What effect did our teasing have on Nick? Was there one day when the taunting and mimicking just 'broke' Jay? What was happening for Paul that led to him abusing substances so frequently? Could we have done more to help him? I doubt I'll ever know the answers to those questions.

But there is another question that I can't shake: What *did our teachers know about Jay's Tourette's or Nick's autism or Paul's drinking?* Were they trained to notice signs of concern in the lives of the students they taught each day? Did they receive information from school management about what was going on in the lives of these boys? Were they equipped with sensible strategies for how to handle the difficult situations that arose?

To my mind, the most exciting development in the field of education over the past decade or so has been the 'discovery' and whole-hearted embrace of the importance of wellbeing within schools. We've seen it in the Health Promoting Schools movement. We've seen it in the Social and Emotional Learning movement. We've seen it in the Positive Psychology and Positive Education movement. We've seen it in the Mindfulness in Schools movement. If schools were ever solely about teaching the 'three Rs' of reading, writing and (a)rithmetic, without doubt we have now moved on. Wellbeing courses are now standard in most Western teacher-training programs. Many schools employ wellbeing coordinators and have sophisticated wellbeing systems to care for the mental health of their students.

Wellbeing is a spectrum with mental *health* at one end and mental *illness* at the other. We all sit somewhere along that spectrum, and indeed our position on that spectrum changes from day to day and week to week. Essentially, schools operate towards the 'healthy' end of the wellbeing spectrum, seeking to promote the skills of good mental health across all students who are healthy enough to be attending school.

As a clinical psychologist, however, my perspective on the wellbeing spectrum is somewhat different. Clinical psychology is the branch of psychology that specialises in assessing and treating mental disorders. Rather than starting at the healthy end of the wellbeing spectrum and looking 'up the line', my perspective has been looking from the opposite end – the *unhealthy* end – and seeking to understand where and how things fell apart. My training was ultimately about how to restore health to those who have crossed the line from having adequately functional mental health to having insufficient health to cope with their basic life tasks without additional support.

While I'm very grateful that we have psychiatrists and clinical psychologists to work within the sphere of serious mental illness, in my own career, I quickly learned that that was not where I wanted to spend my efforts. The idea of sitting in a clinic and waiting until people's lives were unravelling became professionally very unsatisfying for me. I was more interested in using my clinical psychology training to change things *upstream* such that these young people were less likely to end up presenting to mental health clinics.

Introduction

There is no shortage of upstream locations that hold immense potential to alter the life trajectory young people, including the functioning of their family of origin, the work of community organisations that provide youth support, the state and national laws that impact young people, the funding to the health and welfare system, and of course directly upskilling young people themselves to make smart choices in the face of their life challenges. For me, however, the destination with the greatest life-changing potential was the 'natural habitat' of all young people – their school.

Responsibility for the mental health of students can't be the domain of school counsellors and psychologists alone. In even the most fortunate of schools, there is only one psychologist or counsellor for every 500 (or so) students. In most schools around the world, this figure is closer to 1:2000 or more. There is no way possible for counsellors and psychologists to have their finger on the pulse of what is happening for every individual student within their community. However, every student in every school worldwide has a set of teachers who spend an entire year, week-in and week-out, forming individual relationships and seeking to develop those within their care. Imagine if each of these teachers was trained to effectively recognise the signs of emerging emotional distress at the earliest stages. Imagine if they were equipped to have compassionate and effective 'first aid' conversations with their students. Imagine if they had a plan for where and how to link these students with suitable early help.

'Imaginings' like these have been formalised into an exciting development in the field of mental health called *mental health literacy*. Mental health literacy refers to a person's knowledge and beliefs about mental health. It includes being able to recognise signs of concern, knowing where and how to find out information about mental health, knowing about the causes and risk factors associated with mental health disorders, being able to promote and facilitate appropriate help-seeking in light of signs of mental disorders, and knowing about the types of intervention that can be helpful for mental disorders. This 'literacy' about mental health is vital in informing how people respond in the face of signs of mental distress – both in themselves and in those around them.

Mental health literacy wasn't 'invented' when I was in high school. I can only wonder how things might have been different for Paul or Jay or Nick if our teachers had been armed with better information with which to notice and respond to what was happening in their classrooms and playgrounds. And what about the young man at the school where I worked who took his

Introduction

own life? Were there signs of concern that we just didn't pick up or act on? Of course, we can't change what has already passed. Guilt or anger about such matters are only helpful to the degree that they inspire us to change how we act into the future.

I now find myself both challenged and inspired to do more to meet the mental health challenges of young people in schools and to equip school staff to do the same. I'm compelled to combine what I know – as a mental health clinician, as an academic researcher, and as someone who has spent over two decades working in schools – to seek to bring positive change. I am convinced that all of us who work in schools have both the privilege and the responsibility to be part of shaping the mental health of all those in our care. That is not to say that teachers should be pseudo-psychologists. But we can all enhance our own mental health literacy and be equipped with some basic mental health 'first aid' skills.

This is not an academic book. I don't want to impart a stack of interesting intellectual ideas that leave you thinking 'that's fascinating' but unable to do anything with them. Rather, this book is a call to action. It is deliberately and unashamedly *practical* with a clear intention to equip you to act – to do something that will make a difference in the life of a young person. I am also aware that school staff are busy. You don't have time to read a thousand-page tome (unless you are teaching *Anna Karenina* as an English text). In writing this book, my intention is to make each chapter no more than a 30-minute read for even the slowest reader. And so, this book is a 'no nonsense' guide to what you need to know about helping students with emotional and behavioural disorders.

In Chapter 1, I will put the case for why teachers need to be well versed in some basic skills to recognise and respond to students in distress. In Chapter 2, we will take a broad-brush look at the question, 'How would I know if a student in my class had a mental health difficulty?' In Chapters 3, 4 and 5, we will dig a little further into the types of difficulties we might expect to encounter in the classroom. Chapter 3 will focus on the so-called 'internalising' disorders of anxiety, depression and trauma, while Chapter 4 will fly over the 'externalising' disorders, including attention deficit hyperactivity disorder (ADHD) and oppositional students. Chapter 5 will then give a brief overview of some of the less prevalent emotional and behavioural difficulties that can commence during childhood and adolescence, including eating disorders, psychotic disorders and bipolar disorder. The aim and expectation of these early chapters is definitely *not* to equip readers with

Introduction

the skills to 'diagnose' students. Rather, I hope to provide just enough detail on the types of presenting signs to alert the conscientious teacher to mental health concerns.

After that, we will look in more detail at how to respond to those students you feel concerned about. In Chapter 6, we will provide a structure for how to talk to a student that you have noticed concerns about, while, in Chapter 7, we will consider more broadly some classroom approaches to teaching students with emotional and behavioural disorders. In Chapter 8, we consider the special challenges of students who are self-harming or experiencing suicidal ideation.

In the final chapter, we look at the highly important and closely related area of self-care for teachers. Without wanting to spoil the plot, the reality is that the better our own mental health is as educators, the better we will be able to assist those students who are experiencing poor mental health. And so, let's dive into this no-nonsense guide to helping students with mental health difficulties. I have no doubt that, equipped with the knowledge and skills in this book, every educator can truly be life-changing in the lives of their students.

Note

1   All references to individual people in this book are based on real-life examples and situations. To maintain anonymity and to best highlight points, names and details have been slightly changed or may be a fusion of stories.

The case for mental health in schools

> **Millie**
>
> Millie is a Year 9 student at Pelican Point High School. At the start of the year, she impressed as a cheerful, popular and capable young student. Unlike many of her peers, she showed a real interest in Shakespeare. Her *Merchant of Venice* assignment in Term 1 was outstanding, leading her English teacher, Ms Everton, to give her an A+ and to believe she had found a real talent. Millie had even asked Ms Everton to read some poems she had written over the summer. Since mid-year, however, Ms Everton has noticed some changes for Millie. Her usual upbeat character has been replaced by a surlier and more withdrawn persona. She has started making snide comments about some of her classmates in such a way that the tone of the class was being affected. More concerning is that Millie has been increasingly absent from class, and when she is present, she usually arrives late and is disconnected. When Ms Everton asked Millie about the progress of her end-of-year assignment, Millie snapped, yelling something like, 'That's all anyone cares about', and then stormed out of the classroom. Driven by a concern for Millie, Ms Everton approached Doug Fairbrother, Millie's homeroom teacher, to ask if there was anything going on for Millie that she should know about. Doug made a flippant comment about being too busy organising the school's sports carnival to have time to ponder the 'unfathomable depths of the emotional lives of teenage girls'. Ms Everton was not reassured, but she didn't know what else she could do.

The remarkable work of teachers

Teaching is an immensely complex and challenging profession. I've spent 25 years watching teachers 'up close and personal', and frankly, I am in awe. I am in awe of the ability to simultaneously instruct 25 young people, all with different motivations, aptitudes and learning styles. I am in awe of the temperament and wisdom required to manage the behaviour of a class of lively young people. And what about the constant pressures from parents and school management to get results – all of which, of course, is measured regularly throughout the year through assessments and exams? There is barely time to take a bathroom break during the school day, as most teachers are spending their non-class time on playground supervision, taking extra classes for absent colleagues or running the lunch-time chess club. And then there's the behind-the-scenes administration – 'Don't get me started on the admin', I can hear you say! It is only the ignorant and ill-informed who think that the school day finishes at 3 p.m. All the teachers I know are coaching a sport team after school or have taken home a stack of marking or are preparing the debating team or are planning their lessons for the coming days or 'all the above'. Without doubt, teachers have more than enough to do already!

And yet, here you are now, reading a book on dealing with the emotional and behavioural difficulties of students. I can already hear your understandable and indignant response: 'And now you want me to look after the mental health of my student too. Surely you must be joking.'

Please don't throw away the book just yet! I hope you'll at least make it through the next few pages while I put the case that this book will actually help you be a better teacher AND reduce the stress of your job. Let's be clear from the outset: *teachers are not mental health professionals*. It is not your job to provide counselling, diagnose, treat or even 'rescue' students with mental health concerns. This book won't ask you do any of those things. However, the painful reality is that, whether you know it or not, and whether you like it or not, you *will* have students in your class with emotional and behavioural disorders. The Millie vignette at the start of the chapter – or countless other scenarios just like it – is playing out in our classrooms every day. And so, we ask the question: 'Why should teachers now be expected to pay attention to the mental health of their students?' I want to give you four reasons teachers need to take student mental health seriously.

Emotional and behavioural disorders impair student learning

Any definition of a teacher's role will involve facilitating the learning of students. The simple truth is that students learn best when they are healthy and happy. Conversely, poor health – including poor mental health – is a significant barrier to student learning. If teachers want their students to learn well, they need their students to be in a good 'headspace'. This is just common sense. But its more than that; it is substantiated by a mountain of research over many decades.

The best evidence in Australia comes from the Child and Adolescent Mental Health and Educational Outcomes Study[1]. This is a highly important study due to its large scale, national focus, and relationship with the Young Minds Matter survey of child and adolescent mental health and wellbeing.[2] The Young Minds Matter study involved a team of researchers carrying out face-to-face interviews with 6310 parents/carers of children aged 4–17 years as well as survey data collected from parents and young people to find out about the mental health of young Australians. In excess of 5000 of the families that participated in this study also consented for the researchers to access their children's NAPLAN data. Australian readers will be familiar with NAPLAN – the Australian government's National Assessment Program – Literacy and Numeracy. NAPLAN tests are carried out on all students in Years 3, 5, 7 and 9. While far from perfect, NAPLAN does provide a snapshot of a student's educational achievement across the five domains of grammar, reading, spelling, writing and numeracy. The findings from this study about the relationship between educational outcomes and mental health are sobering. Students with mental disorders scored lower than students with no mental disorder in *all* test domains across *all* years assessed. While highly concerning, this result is not unexpected and concurs with other international research.[3]

It is important to note that reduced educational attainment doesn't just refer to scores on tests. Perhaps more concerning are the consistent findings that young people with mental disorders are at greater risk for grade repetition and absenteeism and, ultimately, for premature school dropout. And so, we come back to our starting point: If teachers want to see students learning and achieving sound educational outcomes, they need to be attentive to the vital role that emotional and behavioural disorders will play in undermining these outcomes.

Emotional and behavioural disorders disrupt classroom processes

Perhaps this section would be more aptly titled 'Mental disorders make my class harder to manage', because that is exactly what happens with many students with emotional and behavioural disorders. Experienced teachers can walk into any class and, within five minutes, pick up which are the 'tricky' students – the impulsive ones, the disruptive ones, the detached and unmotivated ones. In years gone by, we may have been resigned to labelling these students as 'naughty' or 'disobedient' and have thought, 'I'll just have to put up with them' or 'It's going to be a long year'. Consider my good friend Steven. It is clear to anyone who knows him that he has ADHD and has *always had* ADHD. He describes his own experience at school as constantly being in trouble for fiddling with any object within reach, jiggling his legs uncontrollably under the table, walking around the class when he was supposed to be sitting, getting distracted by even the slightest disturbance in class (or even just in his own thoughts), and regularly losing everything that he was meant not to lose. The better teachers found ways to connect with and instruct Steven that weren't coercive or negative. However, it is these kids, the kids just like Steven, that we now recognise as having a 'disorder'.

I don't use the word 'disorder' here to label and stigmatise students. In fact, as far as mental health clinicians go, I'm a very 'non-diagnosey' (I know that's not a real word, but you get the idea) psychologist. However, I use this term intentionally because I want to indicate that the students who are the focus of this book are the 20% of young people who experience something that is categorically different, that is more extreme and pervasive than the temporary and comparatively minor 'difficulties' that the 80% of their 'un-disordered' peers experience. And so, for the remainder of this book, I will continue to use the terms 'emotional and behavioural disorders' to describe the problems these students have.

At this point, a very reasonable question to ask is, 'How could I tell if a student has one of these *disorders* or whether they are just high-spirited or impetuous or reserved or whatever?' We are going to investigate that point in some detail in Chapter 2. For now, there are two key points to make. Firstly, there are students in our classes who are more than just active or disinterested or rebellious; they have recognisable disorders that not only make them difficult to teach but can disrupt the entire class environment. Secondly, with a little knowledge, teachers can be equipped with strategies to manage these students – and also be part of a process to ensure that these kids get additional help when it is required. I highly suspect that anyone who taught my friend Steven would have been desperate for any such ideas.

Students with emotional and behavioural disorders are stressful to teach

Disruptive, distracted, unresponsive and off-task students not only disturb class processes but can be highly challenging to the teacher who must manage the class. Teaching is a highly stressful profession. This has been demonstrated by many decades of research. Over the years, academics have sought to carefully identify and describe the sources of teacher stress. The 'usual suspects' include the volume of work, managing the administrative tasks, and satisfying the many stakeholders who all take an interest in the role and performance of the classroom teacher. But amongst all the stressors, one common theme – drawn from data from countries across the globe – is the contribution of having to managing difficult student situations.

This is perhaps best demonstrated by the ongoing Teaching and Learning International Survey (TALIS). Every five years, the Organisation for Economic Co-operation and Development (OECD) surveys approximately 250,000 teachers from 15,000 schools across 48 different countries for the TALIS. The aim of the survey is to provide an opportunity for teachers and principals to give their perspective on the state of education within their own countries, including the systems in which they work and the successes and challenges that they face. No one will be surprised to hear that stress related to student behaviour features as a prominent source of stress in this study. In relation to Australian figures, the most recent TALIS report found that 28% of Australian teachers responded 'quite a bit' or 'a lot' to maintaining classroom discipline being a source of stress, while 13% responded similarly to 'being intimidated or verbally abused by students'.[4] Within a context of high teacher burnout and attrition, it is vital that the profession broadly – and each teacher individually – take this stress seriously and enact steps to minimise the negative impacts of the job on wellbeing. Being better equipped to manage students with emotional and behavioural disorders is one surefire way to address at least one of the important sources of teacher stress and burnout.

Compassion

Before finishing this section on why it is important for teachers to be 'literate' in the ways of mental health, I want to offer one slightly more noble motivator that just about every teacher I know has in abundance – *basic human compassion*. The Institute of Education at the highly regarded University College London is one of the largest providers of teacher training in the United Kingdom. Researchers there were interested to better understand what motivated people to enter the teaching profession – and what motivated them to leave. They asked their most recent five-year cohort of education graduates to indicate from a given list their motivations for becoming a teacher. Two responses stood head and shoulders above the rest: 'wanting to make a difference' (69%) and 'wanting to work with young people' (64%). By some distance, the runners up included some other familiar motivators, such as having a 'love of subject' (50%) and being 'inspired by own teachers' (38%).[5] This is a highly important point to reflect on: *teachers get into teaching because they want to make a difference in the lives of young people.* Most schools have a generous cohort of students who are bright, healthy, motivated, well supported by a caring family, and, overall, on a steady path to success within and beyond school. Clearly, fantastic teachers will help this journey, but these students will likely achieve success even with only 'moderately fantastic' teachers. However, my strong hope is that this desire to make a difference in the lives of young people will especially be directed to help those students for whom life circumstances provide a less certain journey on their path into adult life – in particular, those burdened with poor mental health.

The mental health crisis

On 10 October 2021, in an expression of solidarity reserved for the most serious of situations, a joint statement was issued in the United States by the American Academy of Pediatrics, the American Academy of Child and Adolescent Psychiatry, and the Children's Hospital Association in which they declared a national state of emergency in children's mental health. Their joint statement refers to an acceleration of mental distress in young people in the decade up to 2020, which was then exacerbated by the COVID-19 pandemic. In their statement, these three child health organisations assert:

> We are caring for young people with soaring rates of depression, anxiety, trauma, loneliness, and suicidality that will have lasting impacts on them, their families, and their communities. We must identify strategies to meet these challenges through innovation and action, using state, local and national approaches to improve the access to and quality of care across the continuum of mental health promotion, prevention, and treatment.[6]

This 'state of emergency' hasn't come out of the blue. Anyone working in schools over the period from 2010 onwards will attest to a surging increase in emotional distress in students over this time. From an academic point of view, this has been compellingly documented by Dr Jean Twenge, Professor of Psychology at San Diego State University.[7] Drawing on a nationally representative sample of American adolescents and young adults (and with a sample size of more than 600,000), Dr Twenge investigated changes in the prevalence of mood disorders and suicide-related outcomes in the years 2005–2017. She found that rates of a major depressive disorder in the 12–17-year-old age group increased a staggering 52% over this time, from 8.7% to 13.2%.

Of course, this is not a unique phenomenon in the United States. Research from around the world all points to growing worry about the rise of mental health concerns in young people.[8] Concern about the rising rates of mental illness among young people has led experts to say that we are facing a 'mental health crisis'.[9]

Teachers as frontline workers

With the emergence of such a crisis, we see the corresponding rise of a new type of frontline worker – the worker who, day-in, day-out, inhabits the natural environment of those most vulnerable; the worker who has power to shape the daily habitat of our youth; the worker who has the privilege and responsibility to form relationships over time with those at risk; the worker who is strategically positioned to first see the earliest signs of deviation off course. As our society considers how we manage the ominous trends in youth mental illness, we discover the emergence, even if a reluctant one, of this new type of frontline worker – the humble schoolteacher.

It seems that now, perhaps more than at any other time in history, the Western world has greatly elevated the status afforded to our frontline workers. Perhaps it started following the heroic scenes of police and ambulance workers running towards the Twin Towers on 9/11. In Australia, each summer brings bush fires of seemingly increasing devastation, and always we see our valiant and self-sacrificial Rural Fire Service on the spot to fight them off. During the COVID-19 pandemic, we developed an appreciation of, and gratitude for, the work of the doctors, nurses and other health care staff who selflessly cared for and guided us through a health crisis unprecedented in our lifetime. Frontline workers are those who are first on the spot when we face some kind of crisis and who, if they can respond to the threat appropriately, can restrict the potential damage across the broader community. This elevation of school personnel as key players in addressing the challenges of the youth mental health crisis is not just me having a grandiose moment.

The 'superpower' of teachers

Governments around the world have been developing strategies to address the growing mental health crisis. In Australia, the federal government has produced The National Children's Mental Health and Wellbeing Strategy;[10] in the United States, the Surgeon General has produced a report entitled Protecting Youth Mental Health;[11] in the United Kingdom, the Department for Children has released a report entitled Promoting Children and Young People's Mental Health and Wellbeing.[12] Each of these reports takes a slightly different approach to how their countries can manage the looming mental health crisis, and yet there is one thing that unifies them all: schools generally, and teachers specifically, have a vital role to play in promoting positive mental health and preventing mental illness. For example, the National Health Commission's National Mental Health and Wellbeing Strategy in Australia rests on four core platforms, one of which is 'education settings'.[13] This strategy declares that schools have three vital tasks to play in combatting the rise of youth mental illness:

- creating a *culture of wellbeing* within schools
- providing *targeted responses* to students with special needs
- having *well-equipped educators*

It is this third point that is the focus of this book. Governments (and parents and academics and mental health professionals) around the world are looking to 'well-equipped teachers' to be frontline workers to hold back this unyielding invasion of emotional distress in children and adolescents. And this raises a vital question: Are teachers 'well equipped' for this task that has now been placed on them? The best people to answer this question are teachers themselves – and they have answered with a resounding 'no'.[14] Unequivocally, teachers report that they didn't feel equipped before the mental health crisis of recent years, and they certainly don't feel equipped now that the stakes and expectations have been raised. Teachers express a clear understanding that they are not psychologists or counsellors, and they are *not* looking be equipped with those type of skills. Rather, their requests can be broken into two simple questions:

1. How would I know if one of my students had a mental health difficulty?
2. If they do, what should I do about it?

Mental health literacy and mental health first aid

In the introduction to this book, I raised the idea of mental health literacy as the knowledge and beliefs that a person holds about mental health. The ultimate aim, of course, isn't that people are 'literate' for the sake of literacy. Rather, the hope is that people will use their mental health literacy to change the way they act towards the young people in their care. The natural extension of mental health literacy is the practice of *mental health first aid*. In schools, we are very familiar with first aid training. We regularly get updated with basic training on anaphylaxis, asthma management, cardiac arrest, strains and sprains, and – in Australia, at least – management of spider and snake bites. For any of us who have been the first person on the spot to attend a student who has sustained an injury or become sick, we are extremely glad for our first aid training to guide our response. We don't for one moment delude ourselves into thinking we are orthopaedic surgeons or cardiac physicians who can treat and cure any of these problems. Rather, we learn some elementary information on how to recognise a problem, how to call for help when required, and what to do while we are waiting for the ambulance.

The philosophy of mental health first aid is no different. It is intentionally simple and rests on the core principles of recognising signs of concern, calling in help, and then enacting basic support in the meantime. In fact, school personnel are now more likely to need training to respond to the mental health needs of students than to the physical health needs. I am very grateful to the work of my Australian compatriots Tony Jorm, Betty Kitchener and Claire Kelly in pioneering the training and resources for what is now the international movement of Mental Health First Aid.[15] And so, this book belongs to the fields of both mental health literacy and mental health first aid. It seeks to promote accurate knowledge about mental health disorders, but, more importantly, it seeks to equip readers to act in ways that make a genuine difference in the lives of students.

In a nutshell

- The rate of emotional and behavioural distress in young people is rising to the degree that we are now facing a youth mental health 'crisis'.
- Like it or not, a significant minority of the students in our classrooms are experiencing emotional and behavioural disorders.
- Teachers need to take these problems seriously, in part because emotional and behavioural disorders impair academic achievement, in part because they disrupt classroom processes for all

The case for mental health in schools

- students, in part because students with emotional and behavioural disorders can be highly stressful for the teacher, and in part because it is just what compassionate people do.
- Teachers have become the 'frontline workers' in the face of this youth mental health crisis, and yet they don't feel equipped for the demands of this role.
- Equipped with enhanced mental health literacy and the skills of mental health first aid, school staff can be empowered to make a genuine difference in the lives of these students.

Digging Deeper

1 Lawrence, D., Johnson, S., Hafekost, J., Boterhoven De Haan, K., Sawyer, M. G., Ainley, J., & Zubrick, S. R. (2015). *The mental health of children and adolescents: Report on the second Australian child and adolescent survey of mental health and wellbeing.* Canberra: Department of Health.

2 Goodsell, B., Lawrence, D., Ainley, J., Sawyer, M., Zubrick, S. R., & Maratos, J. (2017). *Child and adolescent mental health and educational outcomes: An analysis of educational outcomes from young minds matter: The second Australian child and adolescent survey of mental health and wellbeing.* Perth: Graduate School of Education, The University of Western Australia.

3 If you want to dig deeper into this, check out Leach, L. S., & Butterworth, P. (2012). The effect of early onset common mental disorders on educational attainment in Australia. *Psychiatry Research*, 199(1), 51–57; Mojtabai, R., Stuart, E. A., Hwang, I., Eaton, W. W., Sampson, N., & Kessler, R. C. (2015). Long-term effects of mental disorders on educational attainment in the national comorbidity survey ten-year follow-up. *Social Psychiatry and Psychiatric Epidemiology*, 50(10), 1577–1591; Riglin, L., Petrides, K. V., Frederickson, N., & Rice, F. (2014). The relationship between emotional problems and subsequent school attainment: A meta-analysis. *Journal of Adolescence*, 37(4), 335–346.

4 Interested readers can access the most recent TALIS report here: Thomson, S., & Hillman, K. (2020). *The teaching and learning international survey 2018. Australian report volume 2: Teachers and school leaders as valued professionals.* Australian Government Department of Education. https://research.acer.edu.au/talis/7. Readers wanting a more comprehensive overview on stress can read McIntyre, T. M., McIntyre, S. E., & Francis, D. J. (2017). *Educator stress: An occupational health perspective.* Berlin: Springer International Press.

5 Perryman, J., & Calvert, G. (2020). What motivates people to teach, and why do they leave? Accountability, performativity and teacher retention. *British Journal of Educational Studies*, 68(1), 3–23. As an addition to our previous section on the stressors of managing difficult student behaviour, this study also asked respondents what they thought would be the biggest challenge about entering teaching. No surprises: 'pupil/student behaviour' was listed as the biggest challenge. Interestingly, as young teachers went on in their careers, student behaviour was seen as a less significant challenge.

6 The joint declaration can be read here: https://www.aap.org/en/advocacy/child-and-adolescent-healthy-mental-development/aap-aacap-cha-declaration-of-a-national-emergency-in-child-and-adolescent-mental-health/

7 Twenge, J. M., Cooper, A. B., Joiner, T. E., Duffy, M. E., & Binau, S. G. (2019). Age, period, and cohort trends in mood disorder indicators and suicide-related outcomes in a nationally representative dataset, 2005–2017. *Journal of Abnormal Psychology*, 128(3), 185–199.

8 For data on Australia, see the Lawrence et al. report cited in Digging Deeper footnote 1; For data on the United Kingdom, see: Newlove-Delgado, T., Williams, T., Robertson, K., McManus, S., Sadler, K., Vizard, T., Cartwright, C., Mathews, F., Norman, S., Marcheselli, F., & Ford, T. (2021). *Mental health of children and young people in England, 2021*. Leeds: NHS Digital.

9 For example, see McGorry, P. D., & Mei, C. (2018). Tackling the youth mental health crisis across adolescence and young adulthood. *British Medical Journal*, 362, k3704.

10 Check it out here: https://www.mentalhealthcommission.gov.au/getmedia/9f2d5e51-dfe0-4ac5-b06a-97dbba252e53/National-children-s-Mental-Health-and-Wellbeing-Strategy-FULL

11 Check it out here: https://www.hhs.gov/sites/default/files/surgeon-general-youth-mental-health-advisory.pdf

12 Check it out here: https://assets.publishing.service.gov.uk/government/uploads/system/uploads/attachment_data/file/1020249/Promoting_children_and_young_people_s_mental_health_and_wellbeing.pdf

13 In case you are interested, the other three focus areas are Family and Community, The Service System, and Evidence and Evaluation.

14 If you want to dig further into how well prepared teachers feel to manage student mental health, you can start here: Kratt, D. (2018). Teachers' perspectives on educator mental health competencies: A qualitative case study. *American Journal of Qualitative Research*, 2(1), 22–40; Mazzer, K. R., & Rickwood, D. J. (2015). Teachers' role breadth and perceived efficacy in supporting student mental health. *Advances in School Mental Health Promotion*, 8(1), 29–41; Shelemy,

L., Harvey, K., & Waite, P. (2019). Supporting students' mental health in schools: What do teachers want and need? *Emotional and Behavioural Difficulties*, 24(1), 100–116.

15 Kelly, C. M., Kitchener, B. A., & Jorm, A. (2016). *Youth mental health first aid: A manual for adults assisting young people* (4th ed.). Melbourne: Mental Health First Aid Australia.

How would I know if a student has a disorder?

> **Kieran**
>
> Year 8 Science has never been Mr McDermott's favourite class. Year 7 was not a problem. He always found that old-fashioned 'scare tactics' were more than sufficient to keep these 'newbies' more or less under control. A piercing look, a raised voice, the threat of being kept back at lunch time – any combination of these tried and true methods was usually enough to keep the noise and rabble to a tolerable level. He had been lucky enough to not have a Year 9 class for some years now, and he found that, by Year 10, most of his students had adequately matured to be almost bearable. And he really enjoyed his Senior classes. But Year 8! They were too old to be intimidated by his faux grumpiness but not old enough to have mastered some of the core elements of basic human civility, like listening or sitting quietly or offering a simple greeting on arrival in the class. And then there was Kieran Battersby. Mr McDermott didn't know what to make of Kieran. He was actually very personable and would usually arrive to class with a smile and, unlike his peers, would offer a friendly 'Hi Mr McDermott' as he entered the room. But from then on, it was near impossible to get Kieran to do anything productive. He couldn't sit in his seat for more than 60 seconds before he had to walk over to chat to a friend on the other side of the class. When Mr McDermott barked at him to sit down, he would then simply continue the conversation by yelling to his mates on the other side of the room without any apparent thought for what else was happening in the class. The most frustrating thing for Mr McDermott was that Kieran showed signs of being quite a

> good student. He seemed to pick up concepts quickly. One day last week, Mr McDermott was so infuriated about Kieran's off-task behaviour that he put Kieran on the spot with a question he thought Kieran would have no chance of answering. To his great annoyance, Kieran gave a commendable answer to the question, to which all the class applauded. Things then came to a head when he found Kieran had taken a Bunsen burner out of the Science stores cupboard, connected it to the gas and was using it to melt a pen. At this point, Mr McDermott totally lost his patience. Safety in his science lab was not negotiable. He ordered to Kieran leave the classroom and issued an after-school detention. At lunchtime, still furious, he called Kieran's mother to inform her of Kieran's behavioural issues and the morning's major safety incident. He was hoping – no, expecting – that Mrs Battersby would understand the gravity of his concerns and give Kieran a serious talking to that evening. Instead, she became angry at him! 'Don't you know that he has a behavioural disability?' she barked.

In my experience, teachers are more than willing to make the required adjustments to accommodate students with emotional and behavioural disorders *if they know that one of their students has a problem*. But how can a teacher know if a student in their class has such a disorder? That is an important question to consider and indeed one that underlies everything else in this book. You are a teacher, not a mental health clinician, and so there is certainly no expectation that you should be able to recognise – let alone *diagnose* – a mental disorder in your students. So, how will you know if a student has a 'condition' that you need to take into account?

There are two answers to this question: the easy way and the hard way. Let's take them one at a time.

Answer 1: The easy way – you'll be told

In a perfect world (yeah, right!), every classroom teacher who has a student with a special need – any special need – would be notified in advance. It's a sign of a well-functioning system when there is a good flow of communication from those 'upstream' in the system to those 'downstream' in the system.

How would I know if a student has a disorder?

Let's take a minute to consider the 'upstream' from the 'downstream' in schools, as this will be an important distinction we make throughout this book. When I refer to those *upstream* in schools, I'm thinking of those staff who hold more senior roles and, in particular, those with specific senior wellbeing roles. These staff will have both additional *responsibilities* for managing students with emotional and behavioural difficulties and usually – hopefully – additional *training* to prepare them for this responsibility. Roles that fall into the 'upstream' category include school psychologists or counsellors, Year Advisors, a Deputy in charge of wellbeing, Special Educational Needs Coordinator (SENCO), Heads of House or a school nurse.[1] Ultimately, these will also include the school's Principal and Deputy Principal. By contrast, those 'downstream' are all other school staff who have interactions with students but are neither trained nor expected to manage more complex emotional and behavioural concerns. Primarily, this will be the classroom teaching staff, but it could also include sports coaches or music tutors or anyone else within the school who has student contact.[2] Keep this distinction in mind throughout the remainder of this book as it will periodically make a difference in how we manage our students with emotional and behavioural concerns.

And now, returning to our main point: in the perfect school, 'upstream' staff will inform 'downstream' staff about any student with a specific emotional or behavioural need. They will have been in communication with the student's parent and/or their external mental health professional, who will have informed them of the student's difficulty, and together, they will have developed an action plan for how the school will manage the student's particular needs. In our perfect-world, smooth-functioning system, when a student has an emotional or behavioural disorder of a nature or magnitude that requires individualised modified classroom management, the classroom teacher could expect to be informed of the nature of the concern and clear information about the modifications required. The two obvious scenarios here are when the disorder significantly impacts the student's own learning and when their disorder presents safety risks for the student or others in the class.

There is, as Mr McDermott discovered, another 'upstream' source of communication – the student's parent. On these occasions, the class teacher may well be the first person in the school to be told about a student's difficulties. My advice to Mr McDermott, immediately following his phone call with Keiran's mother, is to inform the Year Advisor or Special Needs

Coordinator or whoever in the school has oversight of Keiran's wellbeing about Mrs Battersby's revelation so that they can then contact Mrs Battersby, confirm her information and then collaboratively develop a school-wide management plan. Hopefully, this will avoid other staff finding themselves in the same awkward predicament that Mr McDermott found himself in.

At this point, we need to make an important detour to ensure we understand a fundamental principle that will underpin every aspect of information sharing for the remainder of this book.

Information sharing, privacy and duty of care

Every student has a right to privacy concerning their personal information. Unfortunately, on occasions, I have overheard teachers discussing very personal details about students in very public places with no apparent regard to the discrete nature of what they were sharing. I can only imagine the sense of embarrassment, shame, despair or justified outrage that a student would feel were they to learn that their personal information had become the topic of staff room conversation or, worse, had spread from staff to the student body. At its core, privacy is a basic human right extended from one person to another. This right applies to children and adolescents just as much as it does to adults. That should be enough reason for school staff to treat all student health information – including mental health information – with the utmost discretion. However, to reinforce this principle, every country I am familiar with has protected this right through privacy legislation, and schools have obligations under these regulations. In Australia, the most relevant legislation is the Privacy Act 1988, underpinned by 13 Privacy Principles. The Privacy Act affords special attention to what it terms 'sensitive information', which is subject to a higher level of privacy protection than other types of personal information. Critical for our purposes here is that health information, including mental health information, is considered 'sensitive'. And so, from a human rights perspective and from a legal compliance perspective, schools need to treat personal information with the utmost respect.

It is not an automatic assumption that a school needs to know about or distribute information about a student's mental health status. In fact, the opposite is true: schools only need to know about a student's mental health status if there is a good reason to know. From my point of view, there are three good reasons why a student or their family may want a school to know about a student's mental health status. There are also three reasons why a school may want to know about a student's mental health status, and, fortuitously, they are the same three reasons. The first is *educational*. If a student has a disorder that is likely to significantly impact their learning, it is very helpful for a school to know about it and accommodate for it. The second is *safety*. If a student is a risk to themselves or to others within that community, the school should be informed so that it can take steps to mitigate that risk and ensure safety. And the third is *compassion*. If a student is experiencing distress during the school day because of a disorder, a family may hope that the school can provide some additional support, and the compassionate school should be only too willing to assist.

If one or more of these conditions can be satisfied, we have a good case for the sharing of information with a school. But this alone does not mean that information can be shared indiscriminately. When can staff share information about a student's mental health status? I want to offer three essential principles to help guide school staff through how to manage information, however it comes to them, concerning students with emotional and behavioural disorders.

Principle 1 – Seek the student's consent

The best way to know if you can share information about a student's mental health information is as simple as asking the student for their permission. You can ask them *who* they want told, *what* they want told, *how* they want it told, and *when* they want it told. Frequently, they will have very clear preferences about these things, and we should be guided by them. Sometimes, I find students don't have clear preferences, and that is fine too. In these situations, I tend to tell the students my own view on the who, what, how, and when questions. Sometimes, they will instantly agree, and sometimes, they have questions or concerns that we need to talk through. Sometimes, they vehemently request that their personal information not be shared, and we must respect this decision too. My preferred approach is to draft communications, perhaps an email or even just a 'script' of what is to be said, with the student. When it comes to sharing critical information about a student's emotional or behavioural status, not infrequently I will co-draft an email with the student that we then co-sign and send together to their teachers. It's about giving students agency in their own lives. Who better to determine what is to be shared than the student themselves? But that is not the only principle at play.

Principle 2 – Consider your duty of care

There is an enormous expectation on school staff to act in ways that discharge their duty of care for students. This duty of care is usually expressed in language such as taking 'reasonable steps' to protect students when there are 'foreseeable circumstances' that could result in a 'risk of serious harm'. Schools are highly adept at considering risk around playground safety, school excursions or school campus visitors. Being mandatory reporters of suspected child abuse or neglect is another expression of discharging this duty. Just as privacy is reinforced by legislation, so duty of care for students is usually enforced through legislation. In my home state of New South Wales, the most relevant law is the Children and Young Persons (Care and Protection) Act 1998, although most jurisdictions will have similar laws. Such laws enshrine the need to act in ways that protect the wellbeing and safety of young people. Importantly, serious emotional and behavioural disorders can leave a student at significant risk of serious harm. In extreme cases, a student with emotional or behavioural disorders may also be a risk to other students or staff within the school. On occasions, then, school staff must consider how to balance a principle of protecting privacy and attending to a duty of care.

Although this brief discussion is inadequate to fully expound on the complexities of this balance, I hope the chapters ahead will help provide some guidance on how to better understand when emotional and behavioural disorders may – or may not – pose a 'risk of serious harm'. There is, however, one final and default idea to hang on to: at the end of the day, the safety, welfare and wellbeing of child or young person are paramount and take precedence over protection of a student's privacy. In the minority of situations where there is a genuine conflict between privacy and safety, safety wins every time.[3]

Principle 3 – Consider the student's age

Clearly, the age of a student makes a difference to their ability to guide the process of information sharing. Don't misunderstand me here: it is just as crucial to protect sensitive data about a 5-year-old as an 18-year-old. The difference is that, in most cases we can assume that an 18-year-old can make informed choices about their personal data in ways that 5-year-olds are not yet able to. Accordingly, the younger the student, the more we need to include the student's parent or guardian in when and how information is shared. In my experience, though, even very young children can still be contributors to the who, what, when and why matters about information sharing. As a final point before we move on, whether liaising with parents or students, it is good professional practice to have explicit and written clarification for all parties about what you agree in terms of sharing information.

As we move through the remainder of this book, please keep these principles about information sharing, privacy, and duty of care at the forefront of your mind. Returning now to our question, 'How would I know if a student has an emotional or behavioural disorder?', we have discovered the easy answer that the information just lands on your lap from upstream. And ideally, it lands with an associated classroom action plan. But there is a second answer to this question – the *hard* way. In my experience, it is this second answer that plays out far too often in schools and that is at the heart of this book. Unfortunately, the hard answer, in the real world, is. . .

Answer 2: The hard way – you'll have to figure it out for yourself

There is a frightening but consistent research finding from many studies around the world that makes me shudder every time I encounter it: about half of young people with emotional and behavioural disorders are *not* receiving treatment. The most widely cited data for this come from the work of Professor Jane Costello, Director of Developmental Epidemiology at Duke University. Professor Costello drew on a nationally representative sample of over 10,000 American teenagers and reported the horrifying statistic that only 45% of adolescent with a confirmed psychiatric disorder had received treatment from any source in the preceding 12 months.[4] The best Australian data are drawn from the Mental Health of Children and Adolescents: Report on the Second Australian Child and Adolescent Survey of Mental Health and Wellbeing study that we met in Chapter 1. Sadly, data from this study are remarkably similar to those from the United States and found that only 56% of students (aged 4–17 years) with an emotional or behavioural disorder had used professional services in the previous year. That is, 44% of young Australian students who needed professional help had *not* received it.

This line of inquiry has opened a related, equally sinister field of research – that is, the *lag in time* from the first onset of symptoms of a mental disorder in a young person to the time when a person actually gets treatment. A meta-analytic study (that is, a study that analyses all the data from previous studies on the topic) on the pathways to mental health services for young people was carried out at McGill University in Montreal, Canada. One of their interests was to investigate the length of delays before young people with mental health concerns reached the help of mental health settings. The researchers refer to this as Duration of Untreated Illness or DUI. Fifteen studies they reviewed had reported on DUI, and there was a diverse spread of duration, ranging from 1 week all the way up to an incredible 45 years! Despite this disparate response, the authors concluded that 'this wide range for DUI is indicative that there are often extremely lengthy delays before the receipt of appropriate treatment' (p. 1029).[5]

What can we draw from this? The inevitable and confronting conclusion for schoolteachers is that many of our students with genuine emotional and behavioural disorders have *never* been diagnosed and are *not* receiving any type of mental health care. For the classroom teacher, this means that there will be *no* information flowing down from 'upstream', and the teacher is going to have to do it the hard way and figure things out for themselves. This will require the teacher to do some serious thinking, but I guarantee that it is well worth the effort, as the earlier we can get suitable assessment and intervention for young people with emotional and behavioural disorders, the more switched on they will be in class and the better they will be able to reach their academic potential. And there are some things that a teacher *can* bring to the 'diagnosis table' that no mental health professional can bring, and that is the daily observation of the student going about their usual activity in their natural habitat.

So, what does the hard way involve? In the remainder of this chapter, I will offer four questions to consider which help tease out which students we should be concerned about. Please remember that I am not for a minute suggesting that it is a teacher's job to do an amateur Sigmund Freud and diagnose a young person with a psychiatric illness. In fact, we'll soon see that these four questions don't give us any information with which to do that. But what these questions do offer is a system by which teachers can better think through the question, 'Do we have a problem here?'

Question 1: Is this student doing something most other students don't do?

Teachers amass a huge number of hours observing students going about their normal daily routine. Even a teacher in their first year on the job will

How would I know if a student has a disorder?

quickly accumulate many hours in the classroom. From this, all teachers develop a keen sense for what is 'normal' behaviour in their students. Maths teachers will be very familiar with the normal curve (a.k.a. the bell curve). It is the graphic representation of what happens when you plot pretty much any human attribute against the frequency of how often it is observed. Consider what happens when you measure how tall people are. A few people are very short, down one end of the bell curve; a few people are very tall, at the other end of the bell curve; but most of us are somewhere in the middle, making up the body of the 'bell' of the curve.

In a similar way, the behaviour of school students can be thought of as attributes with a frequency that lies along a bell curve. For example, how often do students raise their hand to answer questions in class? Some kids will throw their hands up all the time, and some kids will almost never offer to answer, but most will lie somewhere in the middle. Students who do things in the common, middle section of the bell curve are probably pretty 'normal'. Students who do things at the extreme end of the normal curve are, at least statistically speaking, 'abnormal'. Consider how often a student calls out in class or how often they are late to class or how much they talk with fellow students or how often they complete their homework or how neat their appearance is or how often they smile or anything else you notice that gets your spider senses tingling. The more that a behaviour falls outside the 'normal range', the more likely it is that something is going on for that student. Mr McDermott was an experienced teacher, and it didn't take him long at all to figure out that there was something about Kieran's behaviour that was 'outside the normal range'. He didn't know what it was; he just knew almost no other kids acted that way.

But position on the normal curve alone is insufficient to say that a student has an emotional or behavioural disorder. A student who *always* gets to class on time and *always* does their homework could have obsessive compulsive disorder, but they could also just be a fantastic and conscientious student. So, let's consider our next question as we dig a little deeper.

Question 2: Is this behaviour having an undesirable academic, emotional or social outcome for the student?

Pretty much all emotional and behavioural disorders, by definition, mess up your life. This happens through either the associated emotional distress (guilt, shame, stress, depression) or other undesirable social outcomes, such

How would I know if a student has a disorder?

as getting poor grades, getting disciplines/detentions at school, getting ridiculed or excluded by peers, being berated by parents or even getting in trouble with the law. In fact, the *Diagnostic and Statistical Manual of Mental Disorders* (which we are going to meet soon) taps into this idea when guiding mental health professionals about when a person meets the criteria to be diagnosed with a disorder. For example, to formally be diagnosed with a major depressive disorder, not only do you need to have symptoms of depression (low mood, sense of worthlessness and so on) but the symptoms must also 'cause clinically significant distress or impairment in social, occupational or other important areas of functioning'.

A related idea is advanced by American psychologist Dr Ross Greene, founder and developer of the approach to managing 'explosive kids' called Collaborative and Proactive Solutions (CPS). Dr Greene makes the simple but profound point that 'kids do well *if they can*'. We will unpack some of Dr Greene's ideas in more detail in Chapters 6 and 7. For now, it is enough to say that kids want to do 'well'. Any of us, when faced with the choice of doing 'well' verses doing 'poorly', would naturally choose the 'well' option. Accordingly, if a student is not doing well – if they are experiencing social, emotional, behavioural or academic problems – it is usually because there is something preventing them from doing so.[6]

Sometimes, it will be easily apparent to a teacher that a student is suffering negative consequences from their behaviour. This will include students who receive poor grades, students who regularly receive detentions or exclusions, or students who are in trouble with the law. Sometimes, however, it won't be quite so easy for a teacher to recognise a student's distress – it will be more 'internal'. In Chapter 3, we will investigate further the clues that point to a student having a so-called 'internalising' disorder. For now, however, the point I want to make is that most emotional and behavioural disorders will, by definition, lead to some form of negative consequence or outcome for the student.

Question 3: Are the usual teacher interventions failing to bring about the desired change?

Experienced teachers have been taught or have developed a repertoire of strategies for managing student behaviour in class. Often, a simple reminder from the teacher is sufficient for many students to stop the undesirable behaviour and recommence the preferred behaviour. Sometimes, the teacher will use a louder or sterner voice. A student who consistently fails to complete work in class might be held back to complete work during the lunch break; a student who consistently makes fun of another student might be given a detention or asked to write an apology. In fact, for most students, even the threat of a discipline by a teacher is enough to send a message that something isn't right, and they need to curb their behaviour.

In the same way that experienced teachers know what type of student behaviour fits within the 'normal' range, the experienced teacher also knows what type of reaction to expect in response to their intervention. Normal interventions are likely to work for 'normal' student difficulties, and so, when they *don't* work for a particular student, it should alert us to the fact that there is something different about that student.

Question 4: Do the signs of concern persist over an extended period?

We all have better days and worse days. We all have fluctuations in our mood or in our stress levels. Over the course of a week or a month or a year, it is normal to see a cycle of better times and worse times. The concern comes when we see a pattern over an extended period or when we see a gradual but steady decline over time. This raises the obvious question, 'How long must a concern persist for us to really take notice?' I don't think we don't need to be worried for a student who has a bad class or even a bad week. As a rule of thumb, though, when we see a persistent pattern almost every day for two weeks or longer, we are starting to get into troublesome territory. This doesn't mean we need to wait two or more weeks before we speak to a student about a concern we are noticing. However, when we see it persisting daily for a fortnight or more, we really should start to take notice.

And so, we have four questions that any teacher can ask themselves about students in their class:

- Is this student doing something most other students don't do?
- Is this behaviour having an undesirable academic, emotional or social outcome for the student?
- Are the usual teacher interventions failing to bring about the desired change?
- Do the signs of concern persist over an extended period?

The 'equation' is simple: the more questions to which you answer 'yes', the more likely it is that a student has some form of an emotional or behavioural disorder. Of course, this is not exactly rocket science – or any science at all. Rather, it is a basic 'skeleton' from which to start teasing out whether a student has a problem. In the next three chapters, we are going to put a little more 'flesh' on these bones by providing an overview of the most common disorders that teachers might expect to find presenting themselves in their classrooms.

Before we can do that, however, we need to make one more quick detour to introduce a key 'tool of the trade' for mental health professionals – the *Diagnostic and Statistical Manual of Mental Disorders* (DSM).

The Diagnostic and Statistical Manual of Mental Disorders

Perhaps you've heard about the DSM? Some people refer to it as the 'Bible' for psychologists and psychiatrists in finding common ground about how we define and describe emotional and behavioural disorders. It was first published in 1952 by the American Psychiatric Association and periodically gets updated to reflect developments in the field of mental health. In fact, since 1952, it has undergone four further major updates, most recently in the DSM-5, which was published in 2013.[7] As one sign of change in my profession, the DSM has grown from 132 pages in the first edition to over 1000 pages in the latest DSM-5-TR. Without doubt, it is a highly significant book in the field of mental health.

But don't misunderstand me – this is not a perfect book. It gets criticised by all sorts of people for all sorts of reasons. There are very robust debates within the mental health field over each revision of the DSM about what changes should be made. It gets criticised for being too reductionistic by seeing people as a 'diagnosis' rather than a person; it is criticised for the role it plays in the health insurance industry in countries that require a diagnosis before any money can be paid to mental health providers. The fifth edition in particular has been criticised for lowering the diagnostic threshold required for diagnosis, such that people now are being diagnosed with mental disorders that would not have qualified in years gone by. It is also not the only system for making mental health diagnoses. The most notable alternative is the *International Statistical Classification of Diseases and Related Health Problems*, published by the World Health Organisation and now in its eleventh edition.

But why this detour about mental health diagnosis – why does this matter for this book? Within this book, we need a way of describing and clarifying emotional and behavioural disorders in a concise and coherent way. While the DSM is far from perfect, internationally, it is the most widely used approach for describing emotional and behavioural disorders and therefore very convenient for our purposes. In the next few chapters in particular, I will use DSM terminology, draw on some DSM definitions and provide the DSM criteria that relate to the mental health difficulties discussed.

And so, armed with this information, we can now dig a little deeper into the world of youth mental health and understand more about the types of emotional and behavioural difficulties our students may experience. Mental health professionals typically divide these difficulties into the broad categories of 'internalising' and 'externalising' disorders. These are not DSM classifications but, rather, are convenient ways to break up the ways in which different problems can present. As the name suggests, internalising disorders refer to those characterised by processes within the self, primarily anxiety and depression. These disorders will be our focus in Chapter 3. By contrast, externalising disorders are characterised by behaviours in the external world that are on display for others to see. In Chapter 4, we will look specifically at the externalising disorders of attention deficit hyperactivity disorder, oppositional defiant disorder and conduct disorder. Chapter 5 provides a summary of some of the less common disorders in young people, including eating disorders and bipolar disorder. Although uncommon, these can be totally devastating in the lives of young people and are important for teachers to have at least some basic familiarity with.

Let me again reassure you, we are not delving into the DSM to equip you to make a diagnosis. We just want to ensure that you've got some basic ideas on the types of emotional and behavioural difficulties that all school personnel are likely to come across in a significant minority of students, so you can be better prepared to say, 'Something doesn't look quite right here'.

In a nutshell

- There are two ways that teachers can discover that a student in their class has a mental disorder. The *easy* way is when you are informed, complete with a neat set of classroom management strategies, by the 'upstream' school wellbeing system. The *hard* and unfortunately common way is when you have to figure it out for yourself based on the behaviour of your students in class.
- Four questions can help the classroom teacher think through whether they have reason be concerned about the student's behaviour:
    - Is this student doing something most other students don't do?
    - Is this behaviour having an undesirable academic, emotional or social outcome for the student?
    - Are the usual teacher interventions failing to bring about the desired change?
    - Do the signs of concern persist over an extended period?

Digging Deeper

1. The nomenclature for school staff that I use will largely reflect my Australian context, but I'm sure you can do the translations for role titles in your part of the world.
2. Teachers, obviously, are the main professional group employed by schools. If you are reading this book as a non-teacher staff member, please forgive my practice in this book of generically referring to school staff as 'teachers'. I'm thrilled to have you on board.
3. I implore every school leader reading this book to ensure that staff in your school are trained in their obligations under both privacy legislation and duty of care, with specific attention to the management of students with emotional and behavioural disorders. Similarly, I hope every school staff member will recognise their responsibility to treat sensitive information about students respectfully and take this book as a motivation to remind or upskill themselves on their legislated duty to balance privacy and safety.

4 You can read it for yourself here: Costello, E. J., He, J. P., Sampson, N. A., Kessler, R. C., & Merikangas, K. R. (2014). Services for adolescent psychiatric disorders: 12-month data from the national comorbidity survey-adolescent. *Psychiatric Services*, 65(3), 359–366.

5 You can dig deeper into this study here: MacDonald, K., Fainman-Adelman, N., Anderson, K. K., & Iyer, S. N. (2018). Pathways to mental health services for young people: A systematic review. *Social Psychiatry and Psychiatric Epidemiology*, 53(10), 1005–1038.

6 I can easily imagine some experienced teachers taking issue with the idea that all kids 'want' to do well, as they recall some students who seem hell bent on failure. To that, my response is to say that surely having a student apparently seeking to do poorly is, of itself, a sign of an unhappy or dysfunctional student. Sadly, wanting to do badly can also be a sign of a young person who has given up hope in their own ability to achieve recognition and reward for the socially acceptable behaviours adults are encouraging, and so they seek recognition and reward through other less productive avenues, such as apparent social popularity through being the class clown.

7 I will refer to and cite the DSM on numerous occasions over the coming chapters. American Psychiatric Association. (2013). *Diagnostic and statistical manual of mental disorders* (5th ed.). Arlington, VA: APA.

3 Recognising internalising disorders

Jasmine

Jasmine Jones had been a reasonably quiet student all year. She was intelligent and seemed well liked by her Year 2 peers. As the year wore on, though, Ms Newton became increasingly concerned. Jasmine was becoming more withdrawn and was smiling less than she had at the start of the year. Although the literacy and numeracy screening suggested she had well-developed basic skills, her academic progress seemed to have stalled along with her general motivation to work. In fact, she was yawning and looking tired in class. Ms Newton was also surprised that Jasmine was gravitating towards seeking her out during lunch breaks. The real clincher, though, happened just before lunch one Thursday afternoon. Ms Newton had promised the class that, if they worked well on the Social Science project, she would let them watch 10 minutes of that new cartoon that all the kids were watching. Personally, she didn't get it. The characters didn't speak and just made indistinguishable vocalisations, but the kids loved it. Only a few minutes into the video, Jasmine became very distressed. She began crying and hyperventilating and then ran out of the room in a panicked state. Ms Newton left the class under the supervision of the Learning Support Assistant and ran after Jasmine. Once safely back in the school office, Jasmine couldn't explain how she was feeling other than to say she felt sick and wanted to go home. Ms Newton called Jasmine's mum to collect her, and Mrs Jones arrived within the hour. Ms Newton took the opportunity to explain to Mrs Jones what she had observed in class and ask Mrs Jones if this type of thing had

Recognising internalising disorders

> happened before. She was surprised about the vague nature of the answers Mrs Jones gave. It almost seemed she was being cautious in her replies. Meanwhile, Jasmine was tugging at Mrs Jones's arm, impatient to leave. During one particularly insistent tug, the sleeve of Mrs Jones's shirt lifted, giving Ms Newton a short but clear glance of what looked like significant bruising on Mrs Jones's left wrist and forearm. Mrs Jones quickly buttoned the shirt sleeve and said she had to leave. On the drive home after work, Ms Newton could not get the day's peculiar series of events out of her mind. What had so upset Jasmine? She hadn't observed any bullying or victimisation from other students. In fact, they were all laughing at the humous scene of the angry cartoon man with zany red eyes and cranky vocalisations making animated gestures with his hands. And then there was the unusual interview with Mrs Jones. Why was she so reluctant to talk, and how did she come to get those bruise marks on her wrist? And at this point, a grim theory began to take shape in Ms Newton's mind.

The hard lesson we learned in Chapter 2 was that, frequently, it will be a class teacher or another school staff member who will be the first to form a suspicion that something 'isn't quite right' for a particular student. We introduced some general questions to help guide our thinking about whether a student's behaviour falls within the 'normal' range. That's an OK start in the process of raising a concern, but it doesn't really give us much information to work with. Before we start raising alarms, it would be helpful to have a little more detail. Fortunately, there is not an infinite number of problems that young people can develop. A wise person once told me the simple but profound truth that 'common things occur commonly'. In the context of a book like this, we can take some reassurance that there is only a limited number of common emotional and behavioural disorders that our students are likely to present with.

In Chapter 2, we also learned that these common problems can be considered within two broad categories: the *internalising* disorders, which are mainly experienced 'internally', and the *externalising* disorders, which are usually more obvious for the outside observer to notice. Another set of terms that are used to categorise these problems is as either 'emotional problems', related to how we feel, and 'behavioural problems', related to how we act.

Before we dive in, I want to take this opportunity to restate one of the mantras of this book, that our aim is not to train anyone to diagnose emotional or behavioural disorders. Rather, we just want to add a little more detail to the types of concerns that we will see in our students. There are three questions that will guide us in the ensuing chapters that are at the heart of what school personnel need to know:

1. How common are these problems? How frequently can we expect to see them within our student body?
2. Are there particular students who are at greater risk of developing particular disorders? Are there ways we can predict which students are most at risk?
3. What are the suggestive signs that someone has one of these disorders? What could school staff notice in the students they work with?

The four 'clues' of emotional and behavioural disorders

To better prepare us to identify at-risk students, it is helpful to consider the experience of emotional and behavioural disorders within four categories. I'll refer these as 'clues' in that they are pieces of evidence that inform us about the possible presence of concerns. They are a hint or an indication that something isn't right. The first clue is **behaviour** – that is, what our students do. This is far and away the best clue for school staff to look out for because we can *observe* the behaviour of students in our class. We can see the hyperactive student who is out of their seat or see the cuts on the arm of self-harming student. The second clue category is **physical and bodily reactions**. Sometimes, these are visible, such as the rapid breathing of the hyperventilating student during a panic attack or the psychomotor retardation (which we'll learn about shortly) of the depressed student. At other times, these physical clues are not so obvious, such as the 'butterflies in the stomach' of the anxious student. The third category of clues is the **thinking** clues – the thoughts that students have. This one presents an obvious problem as we *can't* see thought processes. We can, however, listen to the words of our students as an expression of their thoughts, or we can ask students to explain their beliefs and views. Students with certain emotional disorders will hold views that are either highly unusual or out of proportion to the situation they are in. Depressed students, for example, may express highly pessimistic views about the future; anxious students tend to overestimate the likelihood of a 'threat' occurring. Our final clue category is the student's **emotions** – what they feel. The internalising disorders are primarily a disorder of emotions. Again, however, emotions fall into the domain of unobservable. Fortunately, like a student's thoughts, we get insights into their emotions as we listen to their words: 'exams are really scary', 'I feel miserable', 'I was terrified'.

These four clues become our *windows* into emotional and behavioural lives of our students. Sometimes, they are open for all to see; sometimes, the clues require more intentional and careful consideration. And so, with that introduction, we are ready to embark in this chapter on our description of the internalising disorders. Specifically, we will consider the presentation of anxiety, depression and trauma.

Anxiety

No doubt we all have some familiarity with anxiety and fear. They are normal and helpful emotions. Psychologists make an important distinction between anxiety and fear. Anxiety refers to the *anticipation of some future threat*, such as an important upcoming exam. Fear describes our emotion *in the face of an imminent threat*, such as encountering a snake on a bush walk. Importantly, fear can be experienced whether the imminent threat is real or merely perceived. While these emotions are normal, they become problematic when they are excessive in nature, are out of proportion to the actual threat faced, and interfere with life functioning. While normal anxiety before an exam motivates us to study harder, excessive exam anxiety is likely to impair our sleep or concentration, thus undermining our exam performance. Similarly, normal fear helps us successfully navigate the snake on the trail while excessive fear leads us to panic and make poor decisions that could threaten our survival. For some people, the anxiety of even encountering a snake becomes a phobia that prevents them from getting out and enjoying a hike.

Just to complicate matters, we need to think of anxiety disorders as being like the Hydra, the serpent with many heads. While we can consider it as one 'beast', it can present with different 'heads' and in different ways for different people. Moreover, different types of anxiety are likely to appear at different stages of life. Our discussion here will consider the five main types of anxiety that present most often in school-aged children – separation anxiety, specific phobia, social anxiety, selective mutism and panic attacks.

Separation anxiety

Borrowing from the DSM-5, we can define separation anxiety disorder as 'developmentally inappropriate and excessive fear or anxiety concerning separation from those to whom the individual is attached'. The classic portrayal of separation anxiety is the 5-year-old child who tearfully refuses to part from their parent at the school gate. In any given year, we can expect around 4–5% of school-aged children to experience separation anxiety. Separation anxiety is more common in children who have experienced over-protective parenting or family dysfunction. It is the most common presentation of anxiety in children under 12 years of age and sometimes, but not always, resolves by the time the young person reaches adolescence. Accordingly, primary school staff are far more likely to encounter separation anxiety than high school staff. These students will display excessive distress when they experience or even just anticipate being separated from their parents or their home. Subsequently, separation anxiety needs to be considered with any students who are school refusing, particularly the younger ones. Separation anxiety might also be a factor in students who are reluctant to attend school camp or other sleep-over events that separate them from their parents or home.[1]

Specific phobia

The DSM-5 describes specific phobia as the marked fear or anxiety about *a specific object or situation*. There is a set of more common stimuli for specific phobia, including animals (such as spiders or dogs), stimuli in the natural environment (such as heights or storms), blood injection injury (including having injections or other invasive medical procedures) or general 'situational' stimuli (such as airplanes or elevators). Not unsurprisingly, the phobic object is actively avoided, or, if it is encountered, it is with intense fear or anxiety. Specific phobias are common in children regardless of sex, with studies suggesting lifetime prevalence rates of 7–10%.[2] Moreover, most young people who have one phobia are more at risk of having multiple phobias. To be diagnosed, the specific phobia needs to last for six months or more. Parents may not think to alert schools to a specific phobia on the basis that the young person is triggered so infrequently. Nonetheless, teachers may witness a very intense fear reaction from student with an animal phobia on a trip to the zoo, in a biology class for the student with a spider or snake phobia, on a school camp for a student with a thunderstorm phobia or during school vaccination for a student with a needle phobia. In younger students, this may be exhibited through tears or tantrums, while, in older students, it more likely presents as direct avoidance.

Social anxiety disorder

Sometimes referred to as social phobia, social anxiety disorder (SAD) is 'the marked fear or anxiety about one or more social situations in which the individual is exposed to possible scrutiny by others' (yep, that's another DSM definition). Extreme social anxiety can be provoked in just about any context where a person interacts with other people, including meeting new people, attending a social gathering, having to talk in front of others or even being observed going about normal daily activities, such as eating or using public toilets (sometimes referred to as paruresis or 'shy bladder'). Different social anxiety sufferers get triggered by different types of interactions, but all experience the same intense fear and anxiety, and all will seek to avoid these situations. Furthermore, a key fear within social anxiety is that of being negatively evaluated by, rejected by or embarrassed in front of other people. Not uncommonly, a person with social anxiety is worried not only about their initial negative evaluation within their interaction but that others will notice their anxiety about this (for example, that others might notice them sweating or their hands trembling or their skin blushing), which then leads to further anxiety. SAD has an average age of onset of about 14 years for all children regardless of sex, although girls have consistently been found to be more likely to have SAD than boys.

Selective mutism

Selective mutism (SM) refers to the absence of speech in social situations where there is an expectation to speak even when the child can produce normal speech in other situations. The most common scenario is the child who can speak perfectly well at home with their parents and siblings but then does not speak at school to their teacher or their peers or does not speak to grandparents or extended family when they visit the family home.

Recognising internalising disorders

SM is not common, with point prevalence (that is, prevalence at any given point in time) usually around 1% of children. It presents equally in all children regardless of sex, and the onset is usually before the age of 5 years. That said, it is frequently when the child commences school, and the expectations to speak across additional social contexts expands, that the real concerns manifest. SM has a very close association with social anxiety with many researchers and clinicians seeing its presentation as driven by social fears. In fact, it is quite common that, as SM resolves through later childhood and adolescence, the young person continues to experience significant social anxiety.

Panic attacks

The final expression of anxiety we will consider is panic attacks. Many of us, perhaps from personal experience, will be familiar with the frightening surge of intense fear that characterises a panic attack. Along with that deep sense of fear come the physiological symptoms of panic – sweating, shaking, shortness of breath, nausea, dizziness, accelerated heart rate, a fear of 'going crazy' or, worse, a fear of dying. Not everyone having a panic attack necessarily experiences all these symptoms, but anyone who has had one knows that the experience is highly distressing and the fear is very real. These attacks may be triggered by any of the other forms of anxiety we have already met but, in senior high school students, are frequently related to stress about school achievement. Young people are often not good at understanding their own experience of panic or being able to make a connection between their symptoms and other anxieties or stressors in their lives. Making things more complex, it is common for people who have had a panic attack to have further attacks triggered simply by their fear of having another panic attack.

Depression

It comes as no surprise that the main theme of having depression is being sad. Really sad. We're not talking here about the normal ups and downs of mood that we all have, or even the fluctuations that are common in emotional teens. When psychologists talk about having a major depressive disorder, we mean feeling depressed for most of the day, nearly every day. Plenty of teenagers I know are not good at being in touch with their own emotional states and won't be great at articulating their own sadness. Depression may be described not using that particular word but perhaps with experiences like emptiness or sadness or hopelessness. There is, however, one sign that is a real 'giveaway' in depressed teenagers – irritability. Depressed teens frequently become cranky, ill-tempered and just plain grouchy.

But there is a second core symptom to be on the lookout for, and that is a markedly diminished interest in all or most activities. Things that used to be fun are no longer fun. Things the young person used to enjoy doing, they no longer want to do. In fact, depressed mood and diminished interest are so core to the experience of depression that a young person (or an adult, for that matter) cannot be considered to truly have a major depressive disorder unless they have experienced one or both of these signs.

After these two signs, there are a further seven symptoms of a major depressive disorder articulated by the DSM-5:

- Significant changes – either an increase or a decrease – in weight and/or appetite
- Significant changes to sleep patterns: having trouble getting to sleep, having trouble staying asleep or having trouble waking up in the morning
- Psychomotor agitation or retardation: OK, here's one of those psychological terms that need some explaining. 'Psychomotor agitation' refers to a restless energy that causes someone to carry out a range of agitated movements that don't serve any particular function, such as restlessly tapping their toes, shaking their legs under the desk or pacing around a room. By contrast, psychomotor *retardation* is a slowing down of actions and thoughts, evidenced by the person appearing sluggish, moving slowly or speaking slowly.
- Fatigue or loss of energy: feeling tired all the time without any other reason to explain it
- Low self-esteem, often characterised by strong feelings of worthlessness or guilt
- Diminished ability to think, concentrate or make decisions
- Recurrent thoughts of death or suicidal ideation: Clearly, this is very scary, and it's something we'll consider in more detail in Chapter 8.

To truly have a major depressive disorder, a person can't just have one or two of these symptoms. They need to experience five or more of them;

they must exist for a minimum of two weeks; and the symptoms must cause significant distress or impairment of functioning, which, for students, usually means their schoolwork is significantly compromised.

How might a depressed student appear in the classroom? They might just look glum over an extended period. In light of difficulties thinking and concentrating, it is near impossible to be depressed and to maintain your work standards, so teachers may notice a student's work quality drop. Students might be tired or sleepy in class or show signs of weight loss over time (or, less frequently, weight gain). Teachers should also listen in to the language of their students. Depressed students' words may give hints of 'it's all too much', 'what's the point?', 'life sucks', 'I'm stupid', 'I'm worthless' or 'nothing is fun'. Once a student becomes very depressed, even getting out of bed or having the motivation to attend school becomes problematic. Accordingly, mental health clinicians will always check for depression in any student who is a school refuser.

Depression is quite uncommon in pre-pubertal children with one-year prevalence rates of only about 1–2%. For these younger children, rates of depression are quite even between the sexes. That all changes with puberty, where studies consistently show that one-year prevalence rates for 13–18-year-olds jump up to about 5–8%. But the story is a little more complex than that with rates of depression being 2–3 times higher in teenage girls than in teenage boys. And to complicate matters further, young people who reach puberty earlier than their peers are at greater risk for not only depression but other difficulties including substance abuse and early sexual behaviour. The implications for teachers are clear. Very few elementary-aged students will experience depression, but, in high school, it becomes one of the most common disorders to look out for, particularly in girls and those who hit puberty early.

As with all psychological disorders, students with a family history of depression will have an increased risk of developing depression themselves. Studies show heritability of major depressive disorder at about 35%, although they may not develop the disorder until later in life.[3] But there remains one further risk for depression – a really important risk factor all teachers should be aware of, namely, adverse life experiences. Think of pretty much any adverse life experience a young person can go through, and there will be research to show that this cohort of young people is at greater risk of depression: divorce and significant family conflict, overly punitive parenting, exposure to physical violence, having a learning difficulty, having a chronic health condition (think asthma, epilepsy, diabetes, cancer or any other chronic health complaint), psychological trauma and so on. From a school perspective, there is one risk factor above and beyond all others that teachers must be aware of: bullying. Being bullied at school (or indeed cyberbullied beyond the school yard) is consistently associated with young people experiencing low mood. And perhaps even more sobering is that school-based bullying, especially in the younger years, has repeatedly been found to predict depression later in life.[4] If there is only one thing that you take away from this chapter, please remember that students who are bullied are at significantly higher risk of developing depression than their non-bullied peers. This is why it is so important that we implement effective, evidence-based anti-bullying programs in our schools.

Trauma

When mental health professionals talk about trauma, we are referring to typical reactions that people exhibit following exposure to a traumatic event. This, of course, raises the question of what constitutes a *traumatic event*. The DSM helps us out here by defining it as 'exposure to actual or threatened death, serious injury, or sexual violence'. The first point to notice is the idea of *exposure*. This can include young people directly experiencing traumatic events, but equally, it can involve them witnessing events as they occur to others. The second point to note is that traumatic events can be *actual* or *threatened*. Sometimes, just the threat of a traumatic event is sufficient to trigger a traumatic response. The core feature of traumatic events, though, is that there is a threat of death or serious injury. Often, these events are one-off, acute experiences, such as natural disasters (think here floods, fires, hurricanes) but also including physical or sexual assault, car accidents, armed robbery, shootings and the like. However, trauma can also result from repeated or chronic events in a young person's life, such as living in an abusive home environment (think here physical, emotional or sexual abuse) or living in a war zone. For some young people, these events can lead to full-blown experience of posttraumatic stress disorder (PTSD). For others, while their symptoms may not reach the threshold to be diagnosed with PTSD, they may nonetheless experience significant emotional and behavioural distress that is sometimes referred to as an *acute stress disorder* or *adjustment disorder*. Regardless of which category best fits a young person, the experience is highly upsetting and will drastically interfere with their ability to fulfil normal life functions.

Exposure to traumatic events is concerningly common in children and young people. Just how common, though, is complex to determine. Benjamin Saunders and Zachary Adams from the Medical University of South Carolina wrote an important paper on the epidemiology of traumatic experiences in childhood in the United States. They reviewed data from five rigorous studies that used sound methodological screening practices with large, nationally representative samples of adolescents in the United States. From the studies they reviewed, they report that 8–10% of teens had experienced *lifetime prevalence* of sexual victimisation (13–17% of girls and 3–5% of boys); 22% had experienced exposure to at least one natural disaster; 38–70% reported witnessing violence; 18% had lost a family member or friend to some type of homicide; and 21% had experienced a 'serious accident', which could include motor vehicle accidents or in other settings.[5] The take-home point here is that it is only the rare and fortunate student who *hasn't* been exposed to some form of trauma by the time they finish high school.

Sometimes, it will be very evident to school staff that students have been exposed to traumatic events, such as in the wake of a natural disaster or a school shooting. Frequently, however, the traumatic event will not be known to school personnel, such as when a student is keeping a secret about domestic violence at home or when there is historical trauma that the school is unaware of. This is the case for Jasmine Jones, from our vignette at the start of the chapter. It is in these scenarios that teachers will need to observe behaviours and listen to language to determine if something isn't quite right.

Regardless of the type of traumatic event a student has been exposed to, the emotional and behavioural responses to such incidents are quite similar. For our purposes, a helpful template of these responses is provided in the DSM description of the symptoms of an acute stress disorder:

- **Intrusive symptoms**: This refers to involuntary, recurrent, and distressing thoughts and/or dreams about the traumatic event. Children may exhibit repetitive play themes about the events or may have frightening dreams, sometimes without even recognising the content of the dream.

Recognising internalising disorders

- **Negative mood**: Acute and traumatic stress is frequently accompanied by low mood and difficulty experiencing positive emotions, such as happiness, satisfaction or loving feelings.
- **Dissociative symptoms**: Dissociation is a disconnection or an altered sense of reality of oneself or one's surroundings. It can include dissociative amnesia, where you can't remember important aspects of the traumatic events.
- **Avoidance symptoms**: These include efforts from young people to avoid distressing memories or thoughts about their traumatic event or efforts to avoid reminders of things that arouse such memories, including people, places or objects.
- **Arousal symptoms**: Examples of affected arousal include disturbed sleep (trouble falling asleep, staying asleep or even waking up), irritability and anger, difficulty concentrating, or an exaggerated startle response. People who have experienced trauma can also become hypervigilant, scanning their environment for the possibility of further threat related to their trauma.[6]

Final thoughts

Before concluding this chapter, I want to make one final point. Although this chapter has focussed on 'disordered' emotions, it is critical to acknowledge that emotions are a good and normal part of the human experience. There is no problem with feeling sad or worried or upset in the face of life's adversities – it's normal. We are not robots. It does not follow that a student who is in tears following a relationship breakup or the death of a grandparent or receiving a disappointing exam grade automatically needs counselling or additional assessment. Sometimes, we all just need a chance to let out some emotion, allow our family and friends to support us through normal experiences, and then move on.

As community awareness of mental health needs increases, we can run the risk of being too quick to pathologise normal human emotions. In fact, there is a term that has been growing in popularity over recent years to describe the gradual creep of psychiatric influence into broader society: *psychiatrisation*. Psychiatrisation is the:

> complex process of interaction between individuals, society, and psychiatry through which psychiatric institutions, knowledge, and

practices affect an increasing number of people, shape more and more areas of life, and further psychiatry's importance in society as a whole.[7]

The risks of increasing psychiatrisation include overdiagnosis and overtreatment, increased psychological burden of being labelled, exploding health care costs, and a general narrowing of what is essentially normal behaviour. This is definitely not what we want to see happen.

And so, as we finish up this chapter and move through the rest of this book, our challenge is to understand that all emotional disorders, and indeed all behavioural disorders, are major departures from the realms of 'normal' that persist for an extended time and cause significant distress and impairment. The focus of this book is on increasing the mental health literacy of school staff but doing so in a way that balances ensuring that those who genuinely need help get it while, at the same time, not getting lured into seeing problems in students that aren't there to be seen.

In a nutshell

- There are four 'clues' that provide a window into a person's mental health: behaviour clues, physiological/body clues, thinking clues and feeling clues. We can't 'see' all these clues, but we can piece together signs of concern to let us know that something 'isn't right'.
- Internalising disorders are those that are primarily a disturbance of our emotions, when normal and healthy emotions become very intense and distressing.
- Anxiety is a common disorder in young people. It is an excessive and intense fear that is out of proportion to the actual threat faced. The most common anxiety disorders in school populations are separation anxiety, specific phobias, social anxiety, selective mutism and panic.
- Depression is an intense feeling of sadness that exists for a prolonged period of time. It is accompanied by various other symptoms,

> including loss of interest in normally enjoyable activities, irritability, low self-esteem, lethargy and difficulty concentrating.
> - Trauma is a common set of 'symptoms' that a person experiences after being exposed to events where they were at risk of actual or threatened death, serious injury or sexual violence. These symptoms include intrusive thoughts, avoidance of things related to the trauma, low mood, dissociation and distressing arousal.

Digging Deeper

1. My colleague Mary Woods and I wrote a paper a few years ago on students who are reluctant school-camp attenders. Separation anxiety is always an important consideration here. If you have concerns about reluctant camp attenders, dig deeper here: Woods, M. C., & Burns, J. R. (2018). School camp refusal and reluctance: The role of the school psychologist. *Journal of Psychologists and Counsellors in Schools*, 28(2), 235–247.

2. If you want to dig deeper here, check out Burstein, M., Georgiades, K., He, J. P., Schmitz, A., Feig, E., Khazanov, G. K., & Merikangas, K. (2012). Specific phobia among U.S. adolescents: Phenomenology and typology. *Depression and Anxiety*, 29(12), 1072–1082; Kim, S.-J., Kim, B.-N., Cho, S.-C., Kim, J.-W., Shin, M.-S., Yoo, H.-J., & Kim, H. W. (2010). The prevalence of specific phobia and associated co-morbid features in children and adolescents. *Journal of Anxiety Disorders*, 24(6), 629–634.

3. Fernandez-Pujals, A. M., Adams, M. J., Thomson, P., McKechanie, A. G., Blackwood, D. H., Smith, B. H., Dominiczak, A. F., Morris, A. D., Matthews, K., Campbell, A., Linksted, P., Haley, C. S., Deary, I. J., Porteous, D. J., MacIntyre, D. J., & McIntosh, A. M. (2015). Epidemiology and heritability of major depressive disorder, stratified by age of onset, sex, and illness course in generation Scotland: Scottish family health study. *PLOS One*, 10(11), e0142197.

4. If you need more convincing of this, see Ttofi, M., Farrington, D. P., Lösel, F., & Loeber, R. (2011). Do the victims of school bullies tend to become depressed later in life? A systematic review and meta-analysis of longitudinal studies. *Journal of Aggression, Conflict and Peace Research*, 3(2), 63–73.

5. To better understand these figures, see Saunders, B. E., & Adams, Z. W. (2014). Epidemiology of traumatic experiences in childhood. *Child and Adolescent Psychiatric Clinics of North America*, 23(2), 167–184. Data will differ from country

to country and across varying research methods, such as the definitions of trauma and the measurement instruments used.

6 If you would like to dig deeper into educating students affected by trauma, I can't think of a better place to start than Dr Judith Howard's book (2022). *Trauma-aware education: Essential information and guidance for educators, education sites and education systems*. Brisbane: Australian Academic Press.

7 This definition is taken from Beeker, T., Mills, C., Bhugra, D., Te Meerman, S., Thoma, S., Heinze, M., & von Peter, S. (2021). Psychiatrization of society: A conceptual framework and call for transdisciplinary research. *Frontiers in Psychiatry*, 12, 1–11.

# Recognising externalising disorders

> **Noah**
>
> Ms Kaihe is a kind and conscientious Year 5 teacher at St Joseph's Primary School. Now into her second year of teaching, she was beginning to feel some degree of confidence and competence in her chosen profession. She was enjoying coming to work each day, her class was working well, and she was most pleased that her efforts to settle some of the more energetic boys had proven quite effective. She felt particularly chuffed when the principal commended her on the degree of professionalism and composure she had shown for someone still early in their career. All was good in 5K. . ., and then Noah arrived. Noah's family had moved into the district halfway through the year, and he had been placed in Ms Kaihe's class. During the first week, he seemed quiet and perhaps even a little withdrawn. During the second week, he started playing football at lunch time with some of the sportier boys. Ms Kaihe was glad to see that he was finding some friends. All that changed in week 3. She was on playground duty during lunch when she heard two boys arguing. She turned to see Noah push Connor to the ground and then kick him in the back. On separating the boys, Ms Kaihe asked Noah why he had pushed and kicked Connor. He denied that he had kicked Connor and instead said that Connor had hit him. Having taught Conner all year, Ms Kaihe found that very hard to believe. On being sent to the principal's office, Noah screamed 'that's unfair' and threw the football at Conner as he stamped off. This was to be just the first of many times when Noah was involved in playground

> scuffles. Ms Kaihe understood that sometimes kids had arguments. What she couldn't accept, though, was the way that Noah would argue the case and sometimes blatantly lie to her face. And it wasn't just in the playground. Over the following weeks, it became clear that he could be prickly in the classroom. On one occasion, he took a ruler from Bethany's pencil case and claimed it was his. Another time, he kicked a chair out from under Rohan just as he was sitting down, causing Rohan to fall and hurt his back. Before too long, other kids didn't want to sit next to Noah. Ms Kaihe moved Noah to the front, right next to her desk. However, when she turned her back to the class, Noah would turn around and throw things at some other students or make rude gestures. The 'energetic' boys that Ms Kaihe had worked hard to settle earlier in the year seemed to be responding to Noah's antics, and the whole class climate was changing – more distracted, more restless, less focussed. Ms Kaihe couldn't believe that just one student could have such a dramatic effect on the whole class. Nothing she tried seemed to make a difference with Noah. That sense of confidence she had been enjoying just a few months earlier was rapidly being eroded. So much for the professionalism and composure that the principal had commented on.

Anyone who has spent any time in schools will have stories of students similar to that of Noah. Some kids just act out, break the rules and misbehave more than others. These are the kids who, if we are honest with ourselves, can be really infuriating to have in class. They disrupt the teaching and learning of others. They are the 'frequent flyers' on the detention and discipline list. They are the ones most likely to get into fights and always seem to be there or thereabouts whenever there is trouble.

While, in this chapter, we are gathering these students up under the tag of 'externalising disorders', there is another term frequently used in the psychological literature that, in many ways, describes them much better – *disruptive behaviour disorders*. These students don't arouse that same sense of sympathy or compassion that anxious and depressed students do. In fact, it can be very easy to not like these students and to feel personally affronted by their behaviours. Once this happens, it is near impossible to bring a calm and objective mindset to their management.

Recognising externalising disorders

In this chapter, we will be learning that there is a group of students whose misbehaviour is sufficiently beyond the range of what can be considered normal that we must treat it as a genuine disorder. Usually, these are behaviours that the students cannot easily control and are not necessarily of their volition. Moreover, if we persist with approaching these students as if they can understand and manage their own behaviour, we run the very serious risk of becoming part of the problem rather than part of the solution.

The diagnostic names of these disorders may well be familiar to us: attention deficit hyperactivity disorder (ADHD), oppositional defiant disorder (ODD) and conduct disorder (CD). We will consider each of these in order and become better able to recognise the signs of each.

Recognising attention deficit hyperactivity disorder

In my experience, most teachers are now reasonably capable at recognising the signs of ADHD in their students. In part, this is because we have been managing ADHD in schools for some time. Most Western countries saw an explosion of interest in ADHD in the early- to mid-1990s. ADHD had been around, under various names, for a considerable period before that, but since the 1990s, schools have been taking ADHD seriously. In part, however, teachers have become good at recognising ADHD because of *how common* it is. Do you remember that, in Chapter 3, we said anxiety disorders were the second most common disorder in children? If you guessed that ADHD was the most common, you were right!

Studies find that 12-month prevalence of ADHD in children is about 6–7%. Importantly, there is a clear difference in prevalence across boys and girls with an almost 2:1 ratio. In fact, the predominance ADHD in boys has become a concern in that we are discovering that some teachers don't even realise that inattentive or hyperactive girls could have ADHD. There is also evidence that prevalence of ADHD is slightly lower in teenagers than in children.

There is a high genetic loading with ADHD. Children with ADHD tend to have at least one parent who also has ADHD. This heritability component is so strong that a colleague of mine who specialises in ADHD commences his assessment interview by light-heartedly asking parents, 'Which one of you has got it?' Having a parent with ADHD can prove both a blessing and a curse. It is certainly beneficial for a child to have a parent who understands and can empathise with their impulsivity or distractibility. On the other hand, unless these parents have worked hard on their own symptoms, they may not be well placed to teach or model the skills required to manage ADHD.

ADHD has two central features: a persistent pattern of *inattention* and/or a persistent pattern of *hyperactivity – impulsivity*. Let's drill down on each of these one at a time. As has become our custom, we will use the DSM-5 as our descriptive guide to these two central features and what we can expect to see in students who have each one.

Inattention

DSM-5 lists nine different symptoms of inattention, which I'll paraphrase here:

- Often failing to give close attention to detail or making careless mistakes, such as with schoolwork or other activities
- Often having difficulty sustaining attention in tasks, such as while reading or while listening during class
- Often not seeming to listen when being spoken to
- Often not following through on instructions or not finishing tasks, such as schoolwork or duties. For example, they may start a task quickly but then lose focus or get side-tracked.
- Often having difficulty with organisation, such as managing tasks that have sequential elements; difficulty keeping belongings in order; or poor time-management skills or being messy and disorganised with their work
- Often avoiding or disliking tasks that require sustained effort over time
- Often losing their 'stuff' – books, pens, keys, uniform, anything
- Often being easily distracted by extraneous things or easily going off on tangents
- Often being forgetful in day-to-day activities

Hyperactivity – impulsivity

DSM-5 also lists nine key symptoms of hyperactivity – impulsivity in ADHD. Again, I'll paraphrase them here:

- Often fidgeting, tapping their hands and feet, or squirming in their seat
- Often leaving their seat and moving around the room even when they are meant to be sitting down
- Often running when they should be walking or climbs when they should be . . . well, not climbing
- Often unable to play quietly. These kids can be noisy!
- Often 'on the go'. Such is the energy of these kids that, over many editions, the DSM has used the descriptor that they seem to be 'driven by a motor'. It can look like constant energy and restlessness.
- Often talking excessively
- Often yelling out in class. Sometimes, this can be calling out answers even before the teacher's question has been completed. Sometimes, it is just yelling out to someone on the other side of the classroom.
- Often having difficulty waiting in line or waiting their turn
- Often interrupting or intruding on others, such as butting into conversations or using someone else's things without asking or receiving permission

There are some key points to note about these descriptions. I hope you noticed the first word for each symptom: 'often'. Any child can and will do any of these things sometimes, but students with ADHD do them often. Next, students don't need to do *all* these things to be considered to have ADHD, but they will do a *majority* of them. DSM-5 stipulates that six or more symptoms in the inattention or the hyperactivity–impulsivity category are required for diagnosis. That is, kids should never be considered to have ADHD on the basis of having just two or three of these symptoms.

There are various other diagnostic 'specifiers' that we don't need to know about for our purposes here. However, there is one that is very important for school staff. What we do need to understand is that there are three different expressions of ADHD. Sometimes, the inattentive symptoms are the most salient for a student. These are students that can appear dreamy and absentminded through their inattention, and we call this the 'predominantly inattentive presentation' of ADHD. Sometimes, the hyperactive-impulsive symptoms are most evident, which we call the 'predominantly hyperactive/impulsive presentation' of ADHD. And sometimes, students can have the whole complement of inattentive *and* hyperactive-impulsive symptoms, which we call a 'combined presentation' of ADHD.

ADHD and medication

Internationally, the most common treatment for ADHD is medication and, in particular, stimulant medications such as Ritalin, Adderall and Concerta. I have lost count of the number of conversations I've had with young people and their families who have expressed concerns about stimulant medications. Initially, these were concerns that long-term stimulant use might stunt a child's growth. Others have expressed concerns that it is wrong to medicate children with amphetamines – that is, 'speed'. Others still have been concerned that, even if the child is hyperactive, they would prefer a naturally energised child than one that has been 'zombified' by chemicals. Some people are generally disinclined to use any medicines, especially for what is essentially a behavioural rather than a medical problem. It is also true that all medicines come with side effects. I have sympathy for all these views. Moreover, it is only natural that, in the face of a new 'diagnosis' – whether that is a formal diagnosis made by a health professional or a concern raised by a teacher about a very active student in class – families will need some time to think through the implications of seeking help.

The reason that I want to discuss medication here is that it is likely that many school staff will have some or all of the same concerns about stimulants that many parents have and that these concerns could be a barrier to helping students who genuinely have ADHD. Put bluntly, teachers who are sceptical about either the diagnosis of ADHD or the role that medications may play in symptom alleviation won't be part of helping their students get further assessment and intervention. It is wise to bring a cautious hesitancy to medicating children for any emotional or behavioural disorder. Moreover, medicine is almost never a first line of intervention for most disorders. However, it is equally wise to keep an open mind for any assistance that might be beneficial for these students.

To those who start with an assumption that students with ADHD shouldn't ever be medicated, I offer four responses. The first is my anecdotal observations over more than two decades that ADHD medications can bring substantial benefits to hyperactive and inattentive students. Second, and of far greater importance, is that over 70 years of research on the efficacy of ADHD medications has found that they can help young people with ADHD. The efficacy of ADHD medication has been extensively researched across a wide range of outcome variables. One of the most compelling studies I have read is from the highly regarded Karolinska Institutet in Stockholm. Researchers captured data from the entire population of graduating students in Sweden across 6 years, totally more than a whopping 650,000 students! Consistent with other studies, they found that school performance of students with ADHD was substantially lower than that of their non-ADHD peers. Of relevance for our topic here, their data unequivocally demonstrated that students with ADHD who received treatment with medicines, even for three months, achieved more positive school outcomes than those who did not receive medication, including the increased likelihood of progressing into upper secondary school and receiving superior grade point averages.[1] Treatment with medicine does far more, however, than just improve school grades. Children diagnosed with ADHD are much more likely in their adult years to suffer from a broad range of adverse life outcomes, including lower tertiary education; greater difficulty staying employed; being more likely to receive public assistance; and being more likely to engage in risky sexual behaviour, have substance abuse problems, sustain injuries or have accidents, have lower income, and suffer premature death. Central to my case here is that treatment with medication mediates these concerning longer-term outcomes.[2]

Third, for those with concerns about the use of 'stimulant' medications (i.e. from the amphetamine family) for the management of ADHD symptoms, there are various other families of medicines available for physicians to consider. Examples include atomoxetine (brand name, Strattera), guanfacine (Intuiv), viloxazine (Qelbree) and clonidine (Catapres). We don't need to understand the differing mechanisms of action for each. Rather, we just need to understand that there are more medicines available than just stimulants. There is often great benefit for a student and parents – especially those sceptical about medication – to meet with a medical doctor to ask their questions and talk through first-hand the pros and cons of medication.

Fourth, even if you remain unconvinced about the merits of medications, there is an argument that sometimes you are better to choose the lesser of two evils. Medicating kids with ADHD may be problematic, but having kids progress through their school years with their ADHD symptoms unchecked can be far worse. Each week, month and year that a student experiences incapacitating ADHD symptoms, there is an increasing likelihood that they will fall behind with their literacy and numeracy skills, experience ongoing peer conflicting, receive more disciplines from teachers and suffer diminished self-esteem.

There are numerous evidence-based non-pharmaceutical treatments available for ADHD, including parent management training, classroom interventions, social skills training and cognitive behaviour therapy. Best treatment approaches will utilise a multi-modal approach. Deciding on what a student's treatment looks like is ultimately not the job of the school. Instead, our job in schools is to do all we can to get our students properly assessed by the qualified professionals, who will then develop the best treatment approach.

Oppositional defiant disorder

DSM-5 defines the central feature of ODD as a 'frequent and persistent pattern of angry/irritable mood, argumentative/defiant behaviour, or vindictiveness'. These are kids who frequently lose their temper, are easily annoyed, are argumentative with authority figures (primarily parents and teachers), refuse to comply with requests, act out of spite and often deliberately annoy others. That is not an attractive 'cocktail' of behaviours and certainly not what you hope for students in your class. Sometimes, these behaviours occur in only one setting, such as at home or at school, but more frequently they are seen across numerous settings.

First signs of ODD are usually recognised during preschool years, but it isn't until mid-childhood, perhaps 6–10 years or even later, that the pattern of behaviour is sufficiently persistent and sufficiently disruptive to trigger parents or teachers to believe that help is required. Like its disruptive behaviours 'cousin' ADHD, ODD is more common in boys than girls with a ratio of 1.6:1.

Conduct disorder

According to the DSM-5, CD is 'a repetitive and persistent pattern of behaviour in which the basic rights of others or major age-appropriate societal norms or rules are violated'. These behaviours can be shown across four different criteria: aggression to people or animals (for example, often bullying, threatening or intimidating other people; initiating fights; being cruel to animals), destruction of property (for example, lighting fires to cause serious damage), theft and deceit (for example, breaking into another person's house or car, shoplifting, lying to others to obtain goods or favours), and serious violations of rules (for example, staying away from home or truanting school). As with all mental health diagnoses, there are minimum time periods over which these 'symptoms' must be evident, and there are prescribed numbers of symptoms that have to be present before a mental health professional will issue a formal diagnosis. The important point to realise is that these young people aren't just the 'mischievous' kids in the school yard. Students with a CD will frequently show extreme behaviours over an extended period that present risk to others and cause significant impairment to their own social and academic functioning. Children in preschool can show early signs of CD, but its onset is more typically in childhood and into early to mid-adolescence. Prevalence studies find that about 3–4% of students will have CD in any given year and that it is more common in boys than girls.

Shifting lenses

There are various lenses through which we can view students with disruptive behaviour disorders, particularly ODD and CD. The first lens is through the effect that they have on us. They 'push our buttons', they disrupt our classes, they challenge our authority, they upset and hurt people we care about, and they can be just plain unpleasant to be around. This is a view that is easy to understand, and, sadly, this is a commonly held view in schools. This view tends to see the child's behaviour as intentional and stemming from bad character. 'He's just a bad kid'. This view also leads us to become frustrated, angry and punitive with the oppositional or disruptive child. Unfortunately, it is also an unhelpful view that is not in harmony with the science of oppositional children.

An alternate lens is one that is more nuanced and better informed by what decades of research has revealed about these kids. This lens doesn't see ODD or CD as caused by bad character or by a student intentionally choosing to be unkind or hostile to those around them. While it is true to say there is much that we *don't* yet know about the underlying causes of disruptive behaviour disorders, it is just as true to say that there is plenty that we *do* know. Studies find that externalising disorders run in families with vulnerability passed on from parents to children. Twin studies show that there is a 'moderate' level of heritability for antisocial behaviours, including oppositional and defiant behaviours. Moreover, children with ODD have been shown to process social information in different ways than their non-ODD peers. For example, they interpret the motivations of other people in a more hostile way than children without ODD. Children with ODD are also the product of the environment within which they have been brought up. Contextual factors such as the child's family, parenting practices, and parent–child attachment as well as the role of peer and school factors also contribute to how oppositional children behave. We don't need to understand all the reasons why children with ODD/CD act the way they do.[3] What we do need to understand, however, is that there are genuine reasons for why they see the world differently and act differently to their non-ODD peers. It is this second lens that provides school staff with a substantially more helpful perspective on how we can approach these children in a way that benefits them while also helping us maintain our peace of mind.

School management of students with externalising disorders

Our purpose in this book is not so much about classroom approaches to managing students with emotional and behavioural disorders but, rather, about providing 'first aid'. It is about recognising the concern and linking the student with suitable external assessment and intervention. Although I am very cautious about diagnosing students with emotional or behavioural disorders, sometimes a diagnosis can be helpful in shifting our lens away from seeing the child with ODD or CD as a bad or nasty child to viewing them as having a genuine but changeable disorder. More importantly, a shift of lens can help us alter our approach from one of impatience or harsh punishment to one of considered and constructive management.

We have learned that medication can play a central role in management of ADHD. By comparison, medicine is not a frontline approach in the management of ODD or CD. Likewise, hours in the therapy room with a psychologist talking about feelings, doing play therapy or learning mindfulness exercises are not the best way to help these students. Instead, the best evidence-based therapies are behavioural and involve responsible adults – parents and teachers – changing the way they manage the child's behaviour. This isn't to say we shouldn't link these students up with external mental health services. They still need assessment and a carefully considered intervention plan. However, what will make the most difference is what parents and teachers do.

So, what are these behavioural approaches, and what do they direct parents and teachers to do? In essence, they adopt the 'changing lenses' approach I am advocating. They aim to *stop* parents and teachers doing certain things and to *start* them doing other things. Broadly speaking, the behaviours to *stop* include yelling, raised voices, threats or harsh punishments. The behaviours to *start* include remaining calm, noticing and praising acceptable behaviours, building positive relationships, teaching pro-social behaviours, and ignoring (to the degree that it is safe) undesirable behaviours. Key to this understanding is that, when adults resort to coercive and punitive responses, they paradoxically reinforce and promote the very behaviours they are trying to eliminate.

Different research groups internationally have developed and tested structured programs based on these types of ideas. One of the most rigorously investigated programs is the Incredible Years Teacher Management Program (TMP), developed by Professor Carolyn Webster-Stratton at the University of Washington.[4] Training in this approach equips educators to

- develop positive relationships with students, particularly those with disruptive behaviours;
- establish clear and predictable classroom rules;
- praise and encourage positive behaviours;
- use incentives to promote compliance and attentiveness;
- ignore and/or redirect inappropriate behaviours;
- teach students to ignore their misbehaving peers;
- implement consequences and 'time out'; and
- teach students prosocial skills of emotion regulation, social skills and problem solving.

This is certainly a set of ideas I would encourage you to investigate. An alternate evidence-based approach to managing students with disruptive behaviours is the CPS approach that we shall explore a little further in Chapter 7.

Comorbidities

Before we move on from the internalising and externalising disorders, there is one final and somewhat depressing point that we need to consider. There is one major risk factor for all the emotional and behavioural disorders that we have met so far. In short, having one emotional or behavioural disorder is a risk factor for a young person having another emotional or behavioural disorder. This is the notion of 'comorbidity' or having two or more disorders simultaneously.

There are some comorbidities that are more common than others. Having one internalising disorder – for example, depression – is a common risk factor for having another internalising disorder, such as an anxiety disorder. Similarly, having one externalising disorder – let's say ADHD – is a risk factor for also having another externalising disorder, such as ODD or CD. But it is more complex than this. Students with internalising disorders are at greater risk of having an externalising disorder, and those with externalising disorders are at greater risk of having internalising disorders. Basically, any emotional or behavioural condition can occur comorbidly with any other.

Let me share two final depressing concepts before we move on to something a little more energising. The first, and of particular relevance for educators, is that learning disorders such as dyslexia or dyscalculia are commonly comorbid with a range of internalising and externalising disorders. This means that we need to be watchful of the mental health of our students with learning difficulties, especially the longer they progress within the education system with a learning difficulty. Second, and perhaps self-evidently, the more comorbid conditions that a young person has, the greater their risk for worse functional outcomes in life, both in the short term and in the long term. If you think that doesn't seem fair, you are right, and yet this is an undeniable reality of developmental psychopathology.

I don't share these miserable realities to deflate us. In fact, the opposite. I hope that this knowledge of comorbidities can *stimulate* us out of any complacency towards students with emotional and behavioural disorders to realise that these students genuinely require expert help. Sometimes, what we see in the classroom is just the tip of the iceberg, and our students have a whole lot more going on under the surface that we don't know about. The more effective we become at recognising concerns and facilitating a pathway to help, the more likely it is that we can be agents of real and long-lasting change in the lives of our students.

In a nutshell

- Externalising disorders are sometimes also known as behavioural disorders or disruptive behaviour disorders because, as the name suggests, they affect the way a young person behaves and are usually disruptive to those around them.
- Attention deficit hyperactivity disorder (ADHD) has two core features – inattention and hyperactivity-impulsivity. To reach a threshold for diagnosis, a student must have *many* symptoms that occur *frequently*. ADHD can be specified as predominantly inattentive, predominantly hyperactive-impulsive or a combined presentation of both types.
- Oppositional defiant disorder is characterised by a pattern of being argumentative, defiant, irritable or vindictive. Like ADHD, symptoms must be frequent and persistent.
- Conduct disorder is a persistent pattern of disregarding the rights of other people and violating societal norms and expectations.
- Comorbidity refers to having two or more disorders simultaneously. A sad reality of psychopathology is that having any emotional or behavioural disorder is a risk factor for having one or more others.

Digging Deeper

1 This is a really interesting study that you can dive into here: Jangmo, A., Stålhandske, A., Chang, Z., Chen, Q., Almqvist, C., Feldman, I., Bulik, C. M., Lichtenstein, P., D'Onofrio, B., Kuja-Halkola, R., & Larsson, H. (2019). Attention-deficit/hyperactivity disorder, school performance, and effect of medication. *Journal of the American Academy of Child and Adolescent Psychiatry*, 58(4), 423–432.

2 If you need convincing of this, or want to investigate further, you can start here: Boland, H., DiSalvo, M., Fried, R., Woodworth, K. Y., Wilens, T., Faraone, S. V., & Biederman, J. (2020). A literature review and meta-analysis on the effects of ADHD medications on functional outcomes. *Journal of Psychiatric Research*, 123, 21–30; Brunkhorst-Kanaan, N., Libutzki, B., Reif, A., Larsson, H., McNeill, R. V., & Kittel-Schneider, S. (2021). ADHD and accidents over the life span – a systematic review. *Neuroscience & Biobehavioral Reviews*, 125, 582–591; Chang, Z., Ghirardi, L., Quinn, P. D., Asherson, P., D'Onofrio, B. M., & Larsson,

H. (2019). Risks and benefits of attention-deficit/hyperactivity disorder medication on behavioral and neuropsychiatric outcomes: A qualitative review of pharmacoepidemiology studies using linked prescription databases. *Biological Psychiatry*, 86(5), 335–343; Hechtman, L., Swanson, J. M., Sibley, M. H., Stehli, A., Owens, E. B., Mitchell, J. T., Nichols, J. Q. et al. (2016). Functional adult outcomes 16 years after childhood diagnosis of attention-deficit/hyperactivity disorder: MTA results. *Journal of the American Academy of Child and Adolescent Psychiatry*, 55(11), 945–952.e942.

3   For those wanting to dig deeper on the aetiology of ODD and CD, I recommend Chapters 4 and 5 of Matthys, W., & Lochman, J. E. (2016). *Oppositional defiant disorder and conduct disorder in childhood* (2nd ed.). Chichester, West Sussex: John Wiley & Sons.

4   The Incredible Years has their own website with further information. You can explore the evidence for this program here: Korest, R., & Carlson, J. S. (2022). A meta-analysis of the current state of evidence of the Incredible Years teacher-classroom management program. *Children*, 9(1), 24.

Other disorders we can expect in schools

> **Casey**
>
> Ms Benstock, fondly known as Ms B, has been a Year Advisor for 20 years. It was a role she loved, but at 60-something years of age ('Don't you dare ask!'), she was thinking it was time to 'hang up the boots'. And she thought she'd seen it all until she met Casey Vlahos. Casey arrived at Dolphin Bay High School in Year 9, having relocated to the coastal town with her family. Casey's mother had explained that the family had moved to get away from an abusive situation with her ex. She hinted, but never quite openly stated, that Casey had been assaulted by the ex. She did say that he was controlling and violent. Casey's father had died when she was 5 years old, and Mrs Vlahos had been in several relationships since then. Casey had seen many mental health clinicians over the years and was diagnosed with anxiety and depression well before moving to Dolphin Bay. Now in Year 10, Casey seemed to be academically capable, but unfortunately her grades didn't reflect her ability. Ms B put that down to a lack of effort and frequent absence from school. Throughout Year 9, her attendance had gradually deteriorated. In Year 10, her attendance had fallen to below 50%. Frequently, Casey came to Ms B's office in tears to make allegations of being bullied by other girls. On investigation, Ms B discovered that Casey was very quick to perceive rejection from others and would respond in quite extreme ways. She had a history of befriending a group only to have a falling out shortly after followed by periods of not attending school and self-harming. One girl claimed that Casey had bashed her one weekend at the beach when Casey thought the girl was hitting on her

Other disorders we can expect in schools

> boyfriend. Ms B had known plenty of anxious and depressed students over the years but none that baffled or worried her nearly as much as Casey. Some days, she seemed happy and upbeat, and then, just one day later, she was in floods of tears and talking about not wanting to be alive. In fact, on various occasions, the school had to phone Mrs Vlahos and ask her collect Casey after she had been found self-harming at school. At first, Mrs Vlahos begrudgingly collected her, but then one afternoon in November she said she had reached her limit, that she didn't want anything more to do with Casey, that she was unbearable to live with, and that the school should just call emergency services. That day, Ms B and the Deputy Principal drove Casey to the Dolphin Bay Hospital. Casey didn't return to school for 6 weeks. When meeting with Casey and her mother before finally returning, Mrs Vlahos gave Ms B a letter from the hospital psychiatrist. As Ms B read the letter, she read the usual things – 'anxiety . . . suicidal thoughts . . . depression' – but as she read on, she came across something that she wasn't familiar with: 'BPD'. 'What is that?' she thought. Her job really had become so complex over the past few years.

We have discovered that mental health difficulties in young people can be neatly summarised as internalising disorders and externalising disorders or, using slightly different terminology, as emotional disorders and behavioural disorders. We've also met the main 'suspects' within these two broad categories: anxiety, depression and trauma as the primary emotional disorders and ADHD, ODD and CD as the primary behavioural disorders. I'd love to be able to report that this neatly wraps up everything we are likely to encounter in the world of youth mental health. If only things were that simple! In reality, there are many other difficulties that our students can and will present with. In this chapter, we will do a 'flyover' of some of these difficulties. Some of them will still fall within our broad categories of internalising or externalising while others don't fit quite so neatly.

There is one good reason why the disorders we address in this chapter don't get their own chapter: they occur less frequently in child and adolescent populations, and, therefore, we are less likely to encounter them in school communities. We can expect that, in every classroom of 25 students, there will be at least one student – and usually more – with an anxiety or depressive disorder or with an attention or behavioural disorder. By comparison, most of the disorders we discover in this chapter may have a prevalence of perhaps only one or two for every hundred students or even less. It would be a mistake, though, to think that their lower frequency also means they are less distressing or less disruptive in the life of a young person. What we will learn in this chapter is that these disorders are amongst the most severe and impactful on the life and learning of the young person affected. Many of the disorders we will meet in this chapter can require hospitalisation, and we will meet the disorder that has the highest mortality rate of all psychological disorders.

As usual, our purpose in learning about these disorders is never to be equipped to diagnose a disorder. Rather, the aim is to have some familiarity with the key features such that we are able to notice signs of concern and to be part of a support team in ensuring these students get timely and professional treatment outside the school as well as compassionate and supportive management within the school. We won't meet every psychological disorder in children and adolescents, but we will focus on the next level beyond what we saw in earlier chapters. Our first stop will be with the eating disorders, followed by bipolar disorder, borderline personality disorder, psychotic illnesses, obsessive-compulsive disorders, and substance use disorders. Our 'stopovers' at each of these destinations will be frustratingly brief. My hope is that you will consider the student body in the school where you work and reflect on which of these disorders you may need to educate yourself about further.

Eating disorders

Eating disorders have a deserved high profile on the psychological disorders landscape. Disorders in this 'family' are related through their disturbance in eating-related behaviours and pathological concerns about body shape and weight. The first two disorders, anorexia nervosa and bulimia nervosa, are most likely quite well-known. The more recent members of the eating disorders family, binge-eating disorder and avoidant/restrictive food intake disorder, are perhaps less well known. Let's meet them one at a time.

Anorexia nervosa (AN) is characterised by restricted food intake to the extent of significantly low body weight, coupled with an intense fear of

gaining weight and an altered perception of one's own body shape or weight.
- **Bulimia nervosa (BN)** is characterised by repeated episodes of eating an excessive amount of food and then recurrent episodes of behaviours to compensate for or prevent weight gain, such as self-induced vomiting, misuse of laxative, or excessive fasting or exercise.
- **Binge-eating disorder (BED)** is characterised by eating a quantity of food within a distinct period of time that is far larger than what most people eat over the same time and the accompanying feeling that you can't control your eating. People with BED may eat even when they don't feel hungry or eat until they feel uncomfortably full, and they frequently feel embarrassed, guilty or disgusted by their own binge-eating habits. Unlike those with bulimia, people with BED don't regularly use compensatory behaviours to accommodate for the extra calories. In mild forms, people may only binge two to three times a week while, in more extreme cases, people can have a dozen or more binge episodes in a week.
- **Avoidant/restrictive food intake disorder** is characterised by a persistent failure to meet appropriate nutritional needs stemming from a lack of interest in eating food or avoiding food based on its sensory characteristics (for example, how it looks, smells or feels) or concern about aversive consequence of eating (for example, choking or vomiting).

It is difficult to make generalisations about the prevalence and age of onset of eating disorders. We can say that eating disorders affect young women at far greater rates than they do young men, but it is wrong to think that eating disorders are exclusively female disorders. More recent studies suggest that eating disorders affect about 3–4% of adolescents. Rates of AN and BN peak in the mid- to late-teens for girls. This means that high school teachers in particular are likely to have students with these disorders in their classes. Eating disorders do occur in children under 12 years of age, but far less frequently than in the teenage years. Some young people are known to be at greater risk of eating disorders, including elite athletes, dancers and LGBTQI+ youth.

There is one statistic that, more than any other, highlights the urgency in ensuring that young people with an eating disorder be referred to professional help. Eating disorders have the highest mortality rate of all emotional and behavioural disorders. Epidemiologists investigate mortality using

Other disorders we can expect in schools

a statistic called the Standardised Mortality Ratio (SMR). This is a ratio of the number of 'observed' deaths to the number of 'expected' deaths. An SMR of 1.0 indicates that the number of observed deaths is the same as the number of expected deaths for a particular cohort. SMRs higher than 1 indicate that the number of observed deaths in the cohort being studied are higher than that expected of the population on average. One large study found that the SMR for AN was 5.35 with BN and BED both also having an SMR well above 1 (1.49 and 1.5 respectively).[1] For people with AN, these deaths mostly result from damage to bodily organs, primarily cardiovascular complications. Tragically, suicide is the other main cause of death related to eating disorders.

School staff are well positioned to notice concerns about students' eating. We might directly hear reports from students of their dieting or body concerns; we may notice themes of concern in their schoolwork; conscientious staff may notice a student's recess and lunch eating habits or have their interest piqued by a student's bathroom visits; or we may just notice a change in a student's body shape over the course of time.

Bipolar disorder

Bipolar disorder is a mood disorder in which, as the name indicates, the sufferer swings between two (*bi*) poles (*polar*). This is the same disorder that was known for many decades as manic-depressive disorder. The name was changed in 1980 by the authors of the third edition of the DSM, who sought to decrease the stigma that had developed around 'maniacs' and to flag that there is more to this disorder than just its emotional poles. From Chapter 3, we already have some familiarity with what the depressive pole looks like. The second 'pole' in bipolar disorder is the experience of a manic episode. DSM-5 described a manic episode as 'a distinct period of abnormally and persistent elevated, expansive or irritable mood and abnormally and persistently increased goal directed activity or energy'. While depression is considered an *internalising* disorder, mania is very much an *externalising* disorder with these periods of increased activity and energy usually being quite obvious to the outside observer. A meta-analytic study carried out by Dr Anna Van Meter at the New York University Grossman School of Medicine found that the most common symptoms displayed by young people with bipolar disorder are

Other disorders we can expect in schools

- increased energy,
- irritability,
- mood lability,
- distractibility,
- goal-directed activity,
- euphoric/elated mood,
- pressured speech (that is, speaking frequently, intensely and rapidly),
- hyperactivity,
- racing thoughts,
- poor judgement,
- grandiosity,
- inappropriate laughter,
- decreased need for sleep, and
- flight of ideas (that is, a rapid succession of thoughts and ideas, usually expressed through hurried speech).[2]

In more extreme cases, people having a manic episode may experience symptoms of psychosis. While we may not see it at school, during a manic phase, people are likely to have a decreased need for sleep and may engage in a range of risky behaviours, including spending sprees, gambling or sexual indiscretions.

One significant change in our understanding of bipolar disorder has been a distinction between two different types of manic episodes. The 'mania' that I described earlier is typical of the 'original' and more severe form of the disease and is referred to as Bipolar 1. In the second type of mania, Bipolar 2, the manic episode is referred to as 'hypomania' with the *hypo* prefix alerting us to the fact that these symptoms are 'under' or 'below' the full experience of mania in Bipolar 1. In hypomania, the manic symptoms are shorter, less extreme and less disruptive and don't include psychosis.

Bipolar disorder in prepubertal children is rare. Its prevalence increases with each year through the high school period, and there is some evidence that it is more common in girls than boys.[3] There are some well-established risk factors for bipolar disorder, first and foremost of which is having a family member with bipolar disorder. In fact, compared to many other emotional and behavioural disorders, bipolar disorder has a very strong genetic component. Having another disorder, particularly depression, anxiety or a disruptive behaviour disorder, is also a risk factor for bipolar disorder. Manic episodes can also be induced by anti-depressant medication, so school staff should keep a close watch on any student they know is commencing medicine for depression. As soon as it is recognised that a student is in the midst of a manic episode, they should be referred for psychiatric assistance and will likely require immediate treatment with mood-stabilising medicines.

Borderline personality disorder

Personality disorders are a family of disorders in which a person has a prolonged, pervasive, and inflexible pattern of inner experience and behaviour that markedly deviates from what is normal in their culture and that causes significant distress or impairment to the sufferer. It is beyond the scope of this book to discuss them all in any detail. There is, however, one personality disorder that is being seen in school-aged students in greater frequency that all others – borderline personality disorder (BPD). DSM-5 describes BPD as 'a pattern of instability in interpersonal relationships, self-image, and affects, and marked impulsivity'. These are students with a long-term history of fallouts and conflicts with other students, mood swings, trouble controlling their impulses and feelings of low self-worth. Many students with BPD self-harm and experience suicidal thoughts. A central feature for many of these students is an intense fear of abandonment, which drives them to act in erratic and at times desperate ways to avoid or cope with the perceived abandonment. Perhaps you recognised many of these features in our vignette of Casey?

BPD is not usually diagnosed in children under 12 years of age but becomes more prevalent through mid- to late-adolescence. Historically, BPD has been considered to be a disorder that affects girls and women more than boys and men, although more recent studies have found that male–female prevalence rates are not significantly different. Like all these more complex psychological disorders, people with BPD frequently have a range of comorbid psychological disorders, the most common of which are anxiety and depressive disorders, sleep disturbances, ADHD, oppositional disorders and conduct disorders.

BPD causes extensive disruption to the life of a young person. This is primarily through the level of emotional distress of the disorder but also through the amount of time attending to the complexity of their social relationships and then the extensive time commitment of receiving therapy. Consequently, these students are at significant risk of academic underachievement and school-dropout. Medicines are not the frontline treatment for BPD, although students with BPD may be on medicines for comorbid conditions. It is best treated through intensive psychotherapy, usually delivered as weekly individual or group sessions. In more extreme cases, particularly when there is acute suicide risk, young people with BPD may require hospitalisation.

Psychotic illnesses

Psychotic illness is the most dramatic of all mental disorders and perhaps represents what most readily comes to mind when we think of the 'mentally ill'. There are five ways in which psychotic illness can expresses itself. *Delusions* are fixed beliefs that a person holds despite there being very clear evidence to the contrary. Common delusions involve a person believing they are being persecuted or having grandiose views about their abilities or attributes. Sometimes, delusions are just plain bizarre, such as thinking aliens are controlling your mind, while other delusions can appear possible although unlikely, such as believing you are being secretly investigated by the FBI. *Hallucinations* are a sensory experience of something that the person perceives as real but which does not have any genuine external stimulus. The most common hallucinations are auditory in nature, whereby a person believes they are hearing voices or sounds. Hallucinations can also take the form of a perceived sights or smells or tastes.

The third expression of psychosis is *disorganised thinking*, usually presented in the form of what the person is saying. A person's speech can ramble, and their ideas expressed are not coherent or connected in any logical or discernible way to the previously expressed idea. Fourth is *disorganised or abnormal behaviour*. The most renowned form of disorganised behaviour is catatonia, where a person may stop moving or stare blankly. Conversely, they may become quite animated and agitated in their behaviour without any obvious goal for their behaviour. The final domain of psychotic illness is *negative symptoms*, referring to a substantial lessening or absence of usual behaviours such as reduction of speaking or goal-directed activity.

Other disorders we can expect in schools

Psychotic symptoms can present themselves across a range of different disorders in children and adolescents. At one extreme is in the context of a full diagnosis of schizophrenia, where symptoms continue for an extended period and cause substantial disturbance to a person's level of functioning. We have also seen that psychosis can be a part of a feature in Bipolar 1 disorder. Thankfully, both these conditions are quite rare in the school-aged population with schizophrenia occurring in less than 1/10,000 children under aged 12 and considerably less than 0.5% of adolescents. It is also important to know that some young people can experience hallucinations or delusions without having a psychotic illness. In fact, such psychotic experiences are surprisingly common with one systematic review reporting that 17% of children aged 9–12 years old and 7.5% aged 13–18 years old experience psychotic symptoms.[4]

The dramatic and highly bizarre nature of acute and florid psychotic episodes makes them very noticeable to even the most untrained observer. Perhaps more important for school staff is to be familiar with the 'prodromal' early signs of an oncoming psychotic episode. These can be quite subtle and difficult to tease apart from some of the normal variations in teenage behaviour or from other less sinister emotional and behavioural disorders. That said, school staff who have developed relationships with the student over time are perfectly placed to notice these prodromal signs. A list of some common prodromal signs is given in Table 5.1.

Table 5.1 Common Indicators of Early Psychosis

- Difficulty with concentration or memory
- Socially withdrawing/increased time alone
- Low mood
- Irritability
- Changes to sleep habits
- Changes to eating habits
- Deterioration in school performance and completion
- Lethargy
- Becoming suspicious
- Unusual ideas or behaviours
- Decreased attention to appearance and personal hygiene
- Personality changes
- Perceptual changes (hearing voices, seeing unusual things)

Obsessive compulsive disorders

When I was training to be a psychologist, obsessive compulsive disorder (OCD) was considered to be a disordered expression of anxiety. While that is still true, there has been a shift in psychological thinking towards a broader view of obsessive and compulsive behaviours such that various other disorders have been brought together under the umbrella of obsessions and compulsions. Accordingly, some body-focussed repetitive behaviours have been grouped within these disorders, such as trichotillomania (that is, hair loss from the repetitive pulling out of one's hair) and excoriation disorder (that is, repetitively picking at one's skin to the extent of causing lesions). Similarly, hoarding disorder (that is, persistent difficulty throwing out one's possessions due to a perceived need to save them) has been classified an obsessive and compulsive disorder. Our focus in this section, however, will be on two disorders that are more likely to present within school populations, namely 'old school' OCD and body dysmorphia. We'll consider these one at a time.

Obsessive compulsive disorder

Let's begin by unpacking these two words, again using the definitions offered by the DSM-5. Obsessions are 'recurrent and persistent thoughts, urges, or images that are experienced . . . as intrusive and unwanted'. Importantly, these thoughts lead to significant anxiety and distress in the sufferer, who then performs particular actions (that is, compulsions) in order to supress, manage or neutralise the anxiety brought about by the obsessions. These actions are often repetitive *behaviours* but, in some cases, can also be *mental acts* that the person believes will in some way will reduce their anxiety. Examples of mental acts include needing to count in number patterns or pray about particular things in response to an obsessive thought or fear. Some common expressions of OCD, even if disordered, have an understandable logic. If you have a fear of being contaminated by germs (the obsession), it makes sense to frequently wash your hands. If you have a fear of being burgled (again, the obsession), it makes sense to check your locks. Other expressions of OCD seem more unusual to the outsider. Some young people, for example, can have obsessive fears of being gay or might have obsessive thoughts of a tabooed sexual nature, such as incest. The problem in OCD is that the compulsion doesn't satisfy the obsession, and so, shortly after, the person is back to washing or checking or whatever. These compulsions can then become overwhelming, and sufferers can spend hours a day on their compulsions.

OCD can develop at any stage of life, but about 20% of OCD sufferers are diagnosed during childhood, and an additional 25% are diagnosed during adolescence.[5] Given the length of time they spend during the day with students, teachers may often be the first to notice signs of compulsions. The most common compulsions in children are excessive checking, ordering or rearranging things, excessive washing, and even excessive reassurance seeking. A child who is frequently wanting to visit the bathroom may have some contamination fears and need to compulsively wash. Some students just get 'stuck' in their own thought patterns and fail to produce work due this 'stuckness'. Teachers may observe students touching or tapping things in an unusual way. Some students may erase and re-write their work many times due to obsessions around neatness or a need for perfection.

Body dysmorphia

Some years ago, while working in an all-boys school, I remember feeling some sense of relief that I was spared the frequent presentation of eating disorders that my colleagues in co-ed or single-sex girls' schools were dealing with. In my ignorance, I had taken the view that concern over bodies was a 'girl problem'. That all changed one afternoon while walking past our school gymnasium and noticing the large number of boys who chose to work out in the weights room after school. I began wondering about the motivation for these boys working so hard on their bodies. Was this driven by a desire for sensible health routines, or was there some greater *obsessive* driver going on for these boys?

Body dysmorphic disorder (BDD) refers to a preoccupation with perceived defects in one's physical appearance – defects that other people either don't notice or would consider only very minor – such that the person becomes significantly distressed and begins to perform repetitive acts in response to their concerns. Like many psychological disorders, symptoms of BDD usually first appear during adolescence and typically focus on a person's concerns about their skin, face (nose, ears, lips, etc.) and hair and the size, shape, and symmetry of basically *any* body part.

Some of the leading research in this area was done by Dr Sophie Schneider at Macquarie University in Sydney, Australia. Contrary to the view that girls and women may be more focused on their bodily appearance than boys and men, Dr Schneider found similar levels of symptom severity across both groups. What does differ is the bodily areas that male and female sufferers focus on with boys being more concerned with their level of muscularity while girls were more concerned about their breasts/nipples and thighs.[6]

It is a mistake to think that obsessing over body parts or appearance is of only minor concern. BDD is highly distressing for the sufferer and frequently becomes a chronic health condition into adult life. Moreover, it is frequently comorbid with a range of other disorders with suicidal ideation and suicide attempts common in individuals with BDD. Due to shame and embarrassment, young people with BDD are unlikely to speak openly about or seek help for their distress.

Along with the growing concern about BDD, we have seen the development of a new field of science called 'cosmetic psychodermatology'. Cosmetic dermatologists are increasingly aware of patients with emotional disorders like BDD presenting for dermatological treatments to manage their perceived defects and are working more closely with psychiatrists and psychologists to avoid interventions that will likely only worsen a person's problems.[7]

Substance use disorders

I wonder what type of people come to mind for you when you consider people with drug and alcohol problems. The old alcoholic sleeping rough on the park bench? The elite sportsperson or corporate highflier who develops a cocaine addiction? The disillusioned middle-aged suburbanite who turns to liquor to numb a sense of meaninglessness and despair? To those who didn't even consider school students in this category, I want to make two simple points. The first is that drug use – and misuse – is very common in young people. Among Western countries, the United States is the most vigilant in monitoring drug use in young people. Results from a recent national survey on drug use and health sponsored by the US Department of Health and Human Services reported that 3.7 million Americans aged 12–17 years (that is, 14.1%) had used illicit drugs in the previous year, and a staggering 7.5% of 12–17-year-olds used illicit drugs or alcohol to an extent that they had a substance use 'disorder'.[8]

The second point is that having *any* emotional or behavioural disorder is a risk factor for developing a comorbid substance use disorder. One large-scale study reported that adolescents with *any* prior emotional–behavioural disorder had higher rates of both alcohol abuse (10.3%) and illicit drug abuse (14.9%).[9] In the absence of receiving professional assistance to manage their emotional distress of disorders, young people commonly 'self-medicate' with a range of substances.

Experimenting with drugs and alcohol has been a rite of passage for many teenagers as they approach their status as adults. Underage drug and alcohol use can never be condoned, but our concern here is not with infrequent or minor use of substances. Rather, substance *use* turns into *abuse* when it becomes a continuing pattern of behaviour that causes significant interference in a person's physical, psychological, social and vocational/academic wellbeing. Substance abuse is particularly detrimental for young people given that such abuse can grossly interfere with the development of their brain during this critical stage of neural growth.

Interestingly, the prevalence of substance use in high school students across many Western countries has actually dropped over the past 15 years. This isn't to say that substance use isn't a problem; rather, there is evidence of an encouraging trend in usage over recent years. We can get some insights into which substances are most problematic by looking at what substances young people are seeking help for. To help us here, the Office for Health Improvement and Disparities in the United Kingdom has released data showing that, of all young people entering treatment in the United Kingdom, 87% reported having a problem with cannabis, 46% with alcohol and 8% with cocaine and ecstasy. Other substances of concern in this report included ketamine and benzodiazepines. There is one substance that has bucked the trend and shown a dramatic rise over the past 10 years: electronic cigarettes. While we don't yet know the long-term physical effects of vaping, it is already very apparent that vaping is associated with increased mental health risk. Accordingly, we should consider that any student who is regularly vaping is likely to have other mental health difficulties.[10]

School staff are unlikely to directly observe students under the influence of substances and even less likely to see them in the act of using alcohol or drugs. School staff will, however, have conversations with, or overhear conversations about, students and their evening and weekend habits. The point to be made here is that caring and compassionate teachers won't make light of discussions about drug and alcohol use or pretend that it isn't a concern. Rather, they can

Table 5.2 Indicators of Problematic Substance Use

• Risk-taking: engaging in risky behaviours while under the influence (e.g. driving, sex)
• Overuse: using more of the substance than was intended
• Tolerance: needing greater amounts of the substance to get the desired affect
• Impairment: substance use is interfering with completing basic life tasks (attending school, completing academic work, etc.)
• Loss of desirable outcomes: substance use is leading to losing other desirable life aspects such as friendships or good physical or psychological health
• Cravings: experiencing strong desires for a substance when not taking it
• Withdrawal: feeling unwell when not taking the substance
• Loss of control: wanting to reduce substance use but not being able to
• Desperation: engaging in acts of desperation (e.g. crime) to obtain substances

initiate a non-judgemental conversation within which they seek to understand the extent of the student's use of substances and their reasons for drinking or drug taking. Table 5.2 lists the indicators of problematic drug use, which can help staff judge whether what they are hearing from students is problematic.

Final thoughts

This chapter has provided a brief introduction to some of the less common but no less concerning emotional and behavioural disorders that our students may present with. As we acknowledged in the introduction, these disorders have the potential to be more disruptive and destructive than the more frequent 'common colds' of mental illness. By noticing small signs and changes in our students, informed and conscientious school staff can be on the forefront of ensuring these students get timely professional help.

The brevity of our discussion on each of the disorders in this chapter is perhaps as unsatisfying for you as a reader as it is for me as the author. I hope this discontent will lead you to further investigation and learning about each disorder, particularly if any of these presentations resonate with students you are concerned for. I will, however, offer this warning. Mental illness is a field in which there are assorted groups of interested parties offering diverse opinions on the causes and treatments for these difficulties. I'm sure I am preaching to the converted when saying that you need to be very careful about how you go about accessing further information about emotional and behavioural disorders on the internet – or indeed anywhere. The best sources of mental health information are the websites of reputable hospitals or universities who draw on well-established evidence to guide their recommendations. If you are looking to investigate more, that's where I'd start.

> **In a nutshell**
>
> - Although not as common as the internalising and externalising disorders described in Chapters 3 and 4, there are many other emotional and behavioural disorders that will present in school-aged children that can undermine their wellbeing and academic progress.
> - **Eating disorders** are characterised by a disturbance in eating-related behaviours and pathological concerns about body shape and weight. The most common are anorexia nervosa, bulimia nervosa, binge eating disorder and avoidant/restrictive food intake disorder.
> - **Borderline personality disorder** is characterised by a persistent pattern of unstable relationships and sense of self, reactive mood, fear of abandonment, impulsivity, and feelings of emptiness.
> - **Obsessive compulsive disorder** is characterised by recurrent, intrusive thoughts and urges (obsessions) that lead a person to perform repetitive behaviours or mental acts (compulsions) in response to the obsessions.
> - **Bipolar disorder** is a mood disorder where a person experiences both a manic (or hypomanic) episode and an episode of depression.
> - **Psychotic disorders** are characterised by the presence of delusions, hallucinations, disorganised thinking, disorganised behaviour and negative symptoms.
> - **Substance use disorders** are characterised by a continued pattern of substance use that causes significant interference to a person's physical, social, emotional or academic/vocational wellbeing.

Digging Deeper

1. Fichter, M. M., & Quadflieg, N. (2016). Mortality in eating disorders: Results of a large prospective clinical longitudinal study. *International Journal of Eating Disorders*, 49(4), 391–401.

2. Van Meter, A. R., Burke, C., Kowatch, R. A., Findling, R. L., & Youngstrom, E. A. (2016). Ten-year updated meta-analysis of the clinical characteristics of pediatric mania and hypomania. *Bipolar Disorder*, 18(1), 19–32.

3. Mitchell, R. H. B., Hower, H., Birmaher, B., Strober, M., Merranko, J., Rooks, B., Goldstein, B. I. et al. (2020). Sex differences in the longitudinal course and outcome of bipolar disorder in youth. *Journal of Clinical Psychiatry*, 81(6), 19m13159.

4. Kelleher, I., Connor, D., Clarke, M. C., Devlin, N., Harley, M., & Cannon, M. (2012). Prevalence of psychotic symptoms in childhood and adolescence: A systematic review and meta-analysis of population-based studies. *Psychological Medicine*, 42(9), 1857–1863.

5. Vaingankar, J. A., Rekhi, G., Subramaniam, M., Abdin, E., & Chong, S. A. (2013). Age of onset of life-time mental disorders and treatment contact. *Social Psychiatry and Psychiatric Epidemiology*, 48(5), 835–843.

6. You can read more about this research here: Schneider, S. C., Mond, J., Turner, C. M., & Hudson, J. L. (2019). Sex differences in the presentation of body dysmorphic disorder in a community sample of adolescents. *Journal of Clinical Child and Adolescent Psychology*, 48(3), 516–528.

7. Husain, W., Zahid, N., Jehanzeb, A., & Mehmood, M. (2022). The psychodermatological role of cosmetic dermatologists and beauticians in addressing charismaphobia and related mental disorders. *Journal of Cosmetic Dermatology*, 21(4), 1712–1720.

8. Dig deeper into this one here: Substance Abuse and Mental Health Services Administration. (2022). *Key substance use and mental health indicators in the United States: Results from the 2021 national survey on drug use and health.* HHS Publication No. PEP22-07-01-005, NSDUH Series H-57. https://www.samhsa.gov/data/report/2021-nsduh-annual-national-report

9. Conway, K. P., Swendsen, J., Husky, M. M., He, J.-P., & Merikangas, K. R. (2016). Association of lifetime mental disorders and subsequent alcohol and illicit drug use: Results from the national comorbidity survey-adolescent supplement. *Journal of the American Academy of Child and Adolescent Psychiatry*, 55(4), 280–288.

10 There is so much to dig into here. I suggest you start with these papers: Hoots, B. E., Li, J., Hertz, M. F., Esser, M. B., Rico, A., Zavala, E. Y., & Jones, C. M. (2023). Alcohol and other substance use before and during the COVID-19 pandemic among high school students – youth risk behavior survey, United States, 2021. *MMWR Supplements*, 72(1), 84–92; Miech, R. A., Johnston, L. D., Patrick, M. E., O'Malley, P. M., Bachman, J. G., & Schulenberg, J. E. (2023). *Monitoring the future national survey results on drug use, 1975–2022: Secondary school students.* Monitoring the Future Monograph Series. Ann Arbor, MI: Institute for Social Research, University of Michigan; Tehrani, H., Rajabi, A., Ghelichi-Ghojogh, M., Nejatian, M., & Jafari, A. (2022). The prevalence of electronic cigarettes vaping globally: A systematic review and meta-analysis. *Archives of Public Health*, 80, 240; Becker, T. D., Arnold, M. K., Ro, V., Martin, L., & Rice, T. R. (2021). Systematic review of electronic cigarette use (vaping) and mental health comorbidity among adolescents and young adults. *Nicotine & Tobacco Research: Official Journal of the Society for Research on Nicotine and Tobacco*, 23(3), 415–425; Data from the UK Office for Health Improvement and Disparities Sourced from https://www.gov.uk/government/statistics/substance-misuse-treatment-for-young-people-statistics-2021-to-2022/young-peoples-substance-misuse-treatment-statistics-2021-to-2022-report

Raising concerns with students

Jenna

Aadil Ibrahim loved teaching art. He only wished he had more time to devote to his own ceramics. Even so, he got great satisfaction from mentoring some of the fabulous young artists at his school. His biggest joy was helping the final-year students with their major works. He wasn't surprised when Jack chose to create a series of photos of the ocean. He knew that the surf was Jack's passion. Likewise, Rayan's decision to screen-print a series of shirts was a perfect combination of his love for print and for fashion. What did surprise him, though, was Jenna's choice. Jenna told Mr Ibrahim that she wanted to work with oil on canvas and had been inspired by the French Rococo painter Louis-Jean-François Lagrenée and, in particular, his work La Mélancolie. Mr Ibrahim knew the work well. It depicted a pensive young woman with downcast eyes, leaning on her elbow and looking, well, melancholic. Mr Ibrahim held back his surprise at Jenna's theme but expressed his usual enthusiasm for students having interests in the topics they wanted to explore and express. In the weeks that followed, however, Mr Ibrahim watched Jenna more closely. Although she applied herself to her work with some diligence, he also noticed a growing detachment from others in the group. He watched as she started sketches of her ideas and then, in frustration, scrunched them up and started again. He knew that the best art came from deep within the heart, but as the weeks went by, he increasingly got the sense that whatever was rising up from within Jenna's heart was not especially happy. He found himself thinking about Jenna one evening, feeling on

---

DOI: 10.4324/9781003367666-7

> edge about what he was noticing. When he mentioned it to his wife, she said, 'You should ask her if she is OK'. It seemed so obvious. Of course, he should just ask her. But then his mind began to fill with doubts. To be honest, he loved talking to students about art but rarely crossed over to speak to them about their own lives. How would you even start that conversation? Was that even his job? And then, all the 'what ifs' started running through his mind. 'What is she doesn't want to speak to me? What if she tells me its none of my business? Or worse, what if she actually says she isn't OK?' Mr Ibrahim didn't sleep well that night.

People choose to become educators because they are 'people people'. By and large, teachers *enjoy* being with and talking to young people. Even better, by and large teachers are *excellent* at being with and talking to young people. This lays the perfect platform for being able to connect with young people about their mental health, right? Unfortunately, there are a few factors at play that can make talking to students about their emotional and behavioural difficulties a little more problematic than most other teacher–student conversations. To begin with, by the time it is evident that you need to talk, there is a good chance that your relationship with the student has already become strained. The reason you need to talk is frequently because the student is not fulfilling certain expectations in terms of either their behaviour in class or their application to their work. These students can be the ones most likely to 'press your buttons' by being surly, disturbing your teaching, disturbing the learning of other students, being disengaged or generally doing substandard work. Within this context, even the calmest teachers become frustrated and short-tempered. In these situations, it is very difficult for the teacher to approach the conversation with an attitude of compassion and patience, and, by the time you need to have the conversation, the student has seen enough of your grumpy side to think, 'I sure don't want to talk to them'.

A second reason why these conversations can be difficult with students is that they are difficult with *anyone*. The weather or the weekend football results or that fantastic new movie are very non-threatening topics. We can all have those conversations. Likewise, talking with students about the lesson content or the funny thing that happened in the playground are standard fare in the classroom. Unfortunately, however, there remains significant stigma around conversations about mental health. Most of us still feel uncomfortable talking about even *normal* emotions with anyone but our closest friends. Opening up a conversation about mental health concerns is a conversation that, for many of us, remains in the 'too hard' basket.

A final reason that these conversations can difficult is that many teachers will question whether talking to a student about their emotional and behavioural concerns is any of their business. In study after study, teachers report that they don't feel trained to manage the complex emotional and behavioural needs in the classroom.[1] Moreover, most teachers report feeling so swamped with the demands of the normal teaching expectations that the idea of then having conversations with students about their mental health needs is just overwhelming. 'Surely you can't expect me to do that too'.

Let's remind ourselves again: there is no expectation that teachers be mental health clinicians, and it is never a teacher's job to provide treatment for a student's mental illness. The unfortunate reality, however, is that students will bring their emotional and behavioural difficulties into our classrooms, and these difficulties will be barriers to their learning – and frequently to the learning of their fellow students. Sometimes, the school wellbeing system will provide classroom plans for those students with known difficulties, but, as we saw in Chapter 2, teachers will frequently be the frontline workers who are the first to notice and manage these difficulties. Teachers need to have a plan for how to have these frontline conversations.

Thankfully, it need not be difficult, and shortly, I will offer a very simple 'formula' for how to have these conversations. But first, we've got to lay the foundation for how to make any such conversation a success. We can't just expect that our students will be comfortable to speak openly about any difficulties in their life, especially if we haven't put in the work over the academic year to get to know them. And so, the best platform from which we can expect open and honest conversations is to establish respectful relationships in advance.

Establishing strong teacher–student relationships

Relationships are at the heart of teaching. Students learn best in the context of good relationships with their teachers. Teachers enjoy their work most when they experience good relationships with their students. This year-long relationship begins in the very first class of the year. Relationships are always a two-way street, but as the adult and 'senior' member of the relationship, teachers have the responsibility to set the tone with their students. Frequently, it is the simple things that can lay the groundwork for establishing good relationships. Consider your answers to these 'relationship builders' in the classroom:

- I know and use the names of each of my students.
- I know something about each student's interests and hobbies.
- I use kind and respectful language with my students, even if I'm feeling stressed and grumpy.
- I am fair and consistent with rules while also being flexible during those times when 'life happens'.
- I am prepared to listen and give the student the benefit of the doubt.
- I regularly look for and take opportunities to notice and praise the things my students do well.
- I tell my students appropriate things about me/my life so they can get to know me while being conscious to not overshare or tell them inappropriate things.

A teacher can do all these things while still maintaining good class control and upholding strong behavioural standards. Doing these things sets the tone for your teaching relationships over the course of the year, but, from my point of view, it also does something far more at the heart of this book: it lays the groundwork for having a more serious conversation with a student if it becomes apparent that there are concerns to be addressed. Such conversations will only happen successfully if the groundwork is already in place. We can't expect a student to have an honest and vulnerable conversation with a teacher with whom there is no pre-existing relationship. The privilege of teaching is that we get an entire year – class by class – to build those relationships.

I often talk to young people about their 'trust' bank accounts. Every time a student does the 'right' thing and behaves in a trustworthy way around the adults in their life, primarily their parents and teachers, they are depositing a 'trust dollar' into the relationship trust account. The more trust they build up their trust account, the more the parents or teachers will trust them into the future. Conversely, every time a young person does the 'wrong' thing, their trust account takes a hit. Exactly the same principle applies for how we relate to our students. In every class that we show respect and care to our students, we are building up trust and goodwill. Day by day, we grow the relationship. For our students who then have or develop emotional or behavioural difficulties, we can approach a difficult conversation knowing that we already have 'credit' in our trust account.

The mechanics of raising concerns

So, let's assume that you've noticed some concerns about a student, and you've got some reasonable pre-existing relationship with the student. That leads us to our next step – the initial conversation where you raise your concern. As highlighted at the start of this chapter, it isn't necessarily an easy conversation to have. Let's now delve into some of the mechanics about how to make it happen.

Find a suitable time and place to talk

Imagine you wanted to talk to a friend about something going on in your life, something important, something personal, something emotional. You don't want other people to be able to eavesdrop or to see if you have some tears. You also know that this type of conversation isn't the sort that you can have in 30 seconds on your way to a meeting. It will need some time for you to be able to explain your situation and for your friend to offer the comfort, wisdom or perspective that you are seeking. In many ways, raising your concern with a student is no different. If you want to get a truthful and thorough understanding of what is going on for your student, you'll need to set up the right context for your meeting. Primarily, this will come down to choosing the right place and the right time.

Requirements for the right place are not that difficult, but it is crucial to getting the desired outcome. The right place just needs to be somewhere that allows for a private conversation, where others can't hear what is being said. A classroom is fine as long as the rest of the class won't be butting in on you. So, too, a quiet place in the playground or even a quiet office or shared space could work if available. Naturally, all the standard protocols about not being alone with a student in a private place apply, so if you do use a classroom, remember to leave the door open with a clear line of sight. There is no perfect time for any conversation, but there are some parameters to think through that make some times better or worse.

- **How urgent is this matter?** The more urgent the nature of your concern, the sooner the meeting needs to happen. Conversely, if your concern is of a minor nature, there is likely no need to rush a meeting.
- **How calm am I feeling?** Have you heard the truism, 'Never ask your mum to brush your hair when she is angry'? If you know you are feeling frustrated or angry, you are unlikely to bring the calm mindset to the conversation that will bring about the best outcome. In such situations, it can be best to sleep on the matter, perhaps talk to a colleague, and then approach it with a fresh and calmer perspective the next day.
- **How much time do I need?** These conversations are not therapy sessions, and there is no expectation that you need to put aside an hour for an intense 'heart-to-heart'. It is also the case that you can't be sure what direction these conversations may go. Consider the worst-case, uncommon, but possible scenario that, during one of these conversations, a student reveals to you that they are having suicidal thoughts or are being abused at home. You can't abruptly end that conversation and leave the student by themselves. Rather, you will need time to ensure the safety of the young person and immediately link them with the suitable support people within your school. While five to fifteen minutes will be plenty of time in most cases, allow yourself some flexibility in case the conversation takes a turn you weren't expecting.

But what do I say?

Our next challenge is to know what to say. To be honest, this is perhaps the most straightforward step of the lot. I want to share with you a simple two-step approach that I've borrowed from American psychologist Dr Ross Greene, who we met in Chapter 2 – and who we will meet again in a little more detail in Chapter 7.[2] For now, though, I want to give you my own take on the two simple statements that he calls 'The Empathy Step'.

Step 1: 'I've noticed that. . .'
Step 2: 'What's up?'
Let's look at these one at a time.

'I've noticed that. . .'

The first part of the discussion is to share your concern with the student using the simple conversation starter, 'I've noticed that. . .', and then

Raising concerns with students

state your concern in a concise and non-emotional way. Here are some examples:

- I've noticed that you've been late to class a lot over the past two weeks.
- I've noticed that you're not asking as many questions in class over the past month as you were earlier in Term 1.
- I've noticed that you've been sitting alone in class for the past few weeks.
- I've noticed that you're not smiling very much this term.
- I've noticed that, since Easter, the quality of your work has dropped off.

There is an important point to recognise here so you don't get yourself in trouble. The things that you notice need to be articulated as *behaviours* that you have seen – that is, things that are objective and observable. By contrast, we don't want you to channel your inner Sigmund Freud by making interpretations or drawing conclusions that aren't there to be made. Let me illustrate with a few examples.

Emma

Emma is in Mr Singh's Year 11 Maths class. She is a good student and is usually 'bubbly' and engaged in class. Over recent weeks, however, Mr Singh noticed that Emma hadn't been smiling much and had started sitting at a desk by herself. Out of concern, Mr Singh resolved to check it out with Emma. In a class that led into the lunch break, he asked Emma to stay back after the other students had left. He approached Emma and said, 'I've noticed that you've been quite depressed lately'. Mr Singh did everything right: he had gotten to know Emma individually, he noticed some changes of concern, he made a time to talk, he said 'I've noticed that. . .'. And then he undid all his good work by making the *interpretation* that Emma was depressed. Maybe Emma was depressed, but maybe she wasn't. There is a degree of risk in making such an interpretation that could backfire. He would have been much better off just saying, 'I've noticed that you've been sitting by yourself lately and haven't been smiling as much as you usually do.'

Hàorán

Hàorán is in Ms McPherson's Year 8 History class. He regularly calls out jokes and put-downs towards other students in the class, at which a group of Hàorán's friends usually laugh or snicker. Fuelled by her frustration at the ongoing taunts, Ms McPherson kept Hàorán back after class, seeking to better understand his behaviour. 'I've noticed that you like playing the clown in front of your friends', she said. Here again, we see a deviation from what had been 'noticed'. Even in her simple sentence, Ms McPherson had made two assumptions which may or may not be correct – first that Hàorán 'liked' what he was doing; second that Hàorán was indeed 'playing the clown' to get the attention of his friends. There is an additional concern with Ms McPherson's response. By using the expression 'playing the clown', she runs the risk of the belittling or offending Hàorán and, in so doing, shutting down the likelihood of any open and honest response. She would have been better sticking with her observations: 'I've noticed that you are calling out comments to other kids in the class quite frequently'.

'What's up?'

The second part of Dr Greene's Empathy Step is equally simple. In light of the observation that you have just made, you ask the question, 'What's up?' In fact, sometimes you don't even need to ask this question. A brief pause after your 'I've noticed that. . .' comment may be sufficient to get your student to respond. However, if they don't, the follow-up is the direct and concise question, 'What's up?' There is nothing magic about the expression 'what's up'. Rather, it's just an opportunity to show your student that you are concerned and that you are interested to understand more about what is going on for them. That's why it is called the Empathy Step. It's all about understanding the young person's concern from *their* perspective. In fact, I have to confess that I don't always use the 'what's up' phrase. For the young people I work with, I find the expression 'What's going on?' or even 'Help me to understand that' are more natural for me yet still have the effect of opening up a conversation. There might be an alternate simple phrase that works best in the context of the students you work with. I wouldn't advise that you tamper with the 'what's up' question too much, though. The main point is that in a simple, non-judgemental way you invite your student to speak so you can better understand what is going on for them.

Consider the Counselling Theory 101 concept that open-ended questions are best for opening up conversations, while close-ended questions tend to shut down a conversation. The question 'What's up?' helpfully requires some elaboration from the student to answer while the closed-ended question 'Is everything OK?' allows the student to give a minimal 'yes/no' answer, and you come away none the wiser.

And, then we reach the climax of the CPS formula – the part where you stop talking and start listening. This conversation is not a lecture or a dressing down or time for you to talk about yourself. Its sole purpose is to help you better understand what is going on for your student so that you are in a stronger place to effectively help them. And so, you listen. You are not there to provide counselling to your student, but it is a great time to use your teacher 'listening skills'. These are the skills that any of us can use when we talk to anyone to help the other person feel 'heard' and accepted. If you don't know anything about these skills, you need to go and read a 'counselling skills for teachers' book. In this book, however, I throw you these brief reminders about good counselling theory:

- 'Attend' to your student. Watch and listen carefully. Stay 100% focussed on their verbal and non-verbal responses.
- Bring your non-judgemental attitude. If they have any reason to think you are criticising them, they will shut down.
- Consider your eye contact. By looking at them, you let them know you are paying attention, but too intense a stare can be unnerving. Sometimes, it is best to mirror what they are doing with their eyes.
- Make encouraging vocalisations such as 'uh huh' and 'I see' and some affirming 'hmmmms' to let them know you are listening.
- Allow silence. Don't feel you need talking all the time.
- Ask clarifying questions that allow you to better understand what the student is saying or feeling. 'What's up?' can start a conversation, but you may need to ask a few more questions related to what is said to help you better understand the student's perspective.
- Summarise back what you have heard. This allows you to check that you have the correct information and lets the student know that you have understood them.

Where do we go from here?

And that's it – you've opened up a conversation about your concerns. It sounds so simple, doesn't it? What can we expect happen now? The 'what's up?' question (or your equivalent) will yield a response and conversation that will fall on a spectrum somewhere between two extremes. Let's look at them one at a time.

'None of your business – everything is fine'

Perhaps the most common and predictable answer, especially from angsty teens, is that everything is fine, they don't need your help, and it's none of your business anyway. Of course, this doesn't necessarily mean that everything is fine or that they don't need help. But it does mean they don't want to talk about it, or they don't want to talk about it now, or they don't want to talk about it with you. We should never be surprised or offended by this response. However, it would be disrespectful to dig deeper when the student is sending signals that they want you to back off. At this point, you are best to thank them for their time, remind them that you care and are happy to talk further should something come up, and then end the meeting. If the 'back off' signals are not too hostile, you could also ask if they would mind you checking in with them again in a week or two.

'I'm so glad you asked. I really need to talk with somebody.'

At the other end of the spectrum – and, to be honest, the far less common response – is for the student to completely open up, pour out their heart and reveal an entire realm of things that are going on in their life, their mind, their family and their relationships. You may get a whole lot more than you bargained for and certainly more than you wanted to hear. Naturally, in this situation, the conversation will go on for much longer than at the other end of the spectrum. It is vital here to remember your role, especially if the student wants to share information that is way 'deeper' than your role responsibility and skillset. Regardless of the content of this deeper information, if genuine concerns are disclosed, the response of the caring teacher is deceptively simple, and that is to facilitate an ongoing discussion between the student and a more suitable 'helper'. We'll explore the process of linking students with appropriate mental health assessment and intervention more in Chapter 9. For the classroom teacher looking to make an initial 'upstream' escalation, the helper will usually be someone inside the school/system, such as a school counsellor or psychologist or perhaps Head Teacher Welfare or SENCO – perhaps even the student's parent(s). But how can you do that?

Raising concerns with students

Let's eavesdrop here on a conversation between Ms Gilman, who initiated a meeting with Calvin after class after noticing that he had seemed distracted and distant over the past month. Calvin burst into tears and, over the next 20 minutes, went into some detail explaining that his parents had been fighting for many months, that his father had lost his job and that his mother's job barely covered their bills, and that he wasn't sleeping at nights and felt tired and miserable every day. While not wanting to leave Calvin in distress, Ms Gilman's knew that (1) Calvin needed more help than she could offer, (2) she had to teach a Year 9 Spanish class in 10 minutes . . . and (3) she hadn't had any lunch yet. She wrapped up her conversation with Calvin as follows:

Ms Gilman	Calvin, thank you so much for sharing all this with me. Things have certainly been tough for you lately. It makes perfect sense to me now why you've been so distant in class. I'm sure you've been trying your very best, but it also seems like everything is just getting overwhelming for you right now. Does that sound right?
Calvin	Yes, Miss.
Ms Gilman	I really want to help you with this, but there are people who know a lot more about things like this than me. I'd would like to organise for you to speak to Miss Nguyen, the school counsellor. Have you ever met her before?
Calvin	No, Miss.
Ms Gilman	I'd like to tell her about the things you've told me so she can help you find a way to cope better at home. Is that OK with you?
Calvin	Can't I just talk to you, Miss? I don't really want to talk to someone I don't know.
Ms Gilman	I'm so glad you feel comfortable to talk to me, but to be honest, Miss Nguyen knows a million times more than I do about these things, and I think she can help you far better than me. I know that she will be very discrete with any information that you tell her. Are you worried about your parents finding out?
Calvin	A little.
Ms Gilman	I can let her know that. As a counsellor, she is very used to talking to kids about all sorts of very private things. Perhaps we could drop over to her office now and see if she is in. Is that OK?
Calvin	I guess.
Ms Gilman	Good man. I know this is scary, but I really think that is the best place for you to get help with this. Her office is down this way.

There are no magic words here, but there are definitely some key *ingredients* when turning the conversation towards linking the student with another helper. Ms Gilman *thanked* Calvin for his openness. By doing this, she recognised that sharing at a personal level takes both internal courage and trust in the other person. Ms Gilman showed her appreciation of this trust. She *validated* both his story and his emotions, thus showing Calvin that she understood the core of what he had told her. She *reassured* him of her desire to help and not just leave him to cope alone. She also reassured him about the information he had shared being treated with discretion. Finally, she *suggested help* in the form of the school counsellor, even though Calvin initially expressed some reluctance. These are all helpful elements to incorporate into the conversation as you steer a student to upstream help.

Assessing risk

Before we move on from this conversation, we need to consider one final component of the helping conversation. As we amalgamate information that we have about a student – from what we've observed and from what we've been told – we need some way of knowing how worried we should be. Ultimately, this comes down to making a risk assessment. Assessing risk revolves around two key questions.

Question 1: What impact could this have on the student's, or somebody else's, life?

This first question revolves around *how serious* this problem could be or become. Answering this involves combing through the information you have to determine the most concerning and impactful aspects. Worst-case scenarios involve students who have made physical and tangible threats to harm themselves or others or who have revealed information that they have been threatened or harmed by others. Your job will be to integrate what you know about this student, their community and young people in general to develop a sense of *how bad* this threat may be. A helpful question to ask the student is 'What is the worst-case scenario here?'

Question 2: How likely is it that this bad thing could happen?

This second question revolves around the *probability* of the bad thing happening. Answering this involves combing through the information you have to ascertain the chances of something bad happening. Sometimes, you will receive information that something bad has already happened, such as self-harm or abuse. Sometimes, you will receive information that the student is considering some action which is highly plausible and possible but has not yet happened. Alternatively, they may tell you that they have been threatened in some way. Again, your job here will be to integrate what you know about this student, their community and young people in general to develop a sense of the *likelihood* of a bad event eventuating. A helpful question to ask the student is 'How likely is it that this could happen?'

The risk assessment then revolves around what you know about the impact and the likelihood of the behaviour of concern. In simple terms, the more impactful the event and the more likely that it is to happen, the greater the risk; the less impactful the event and the less likely that it is to happen, the less the risk. Reduced to two basic questions, the risk assessment sounds so simple.

The reality, of course, is that risk assessments are complex, and getting them wrong could literally prove to be the difference between life and death. Because of this, I suspect most 'risk managers' in schools won't want school staff to read this book and then falsely believe they are equipped to make a risk assessment of highly distressed students. Instead, the safe and sensible option, especially for any downstream staff, is to escalate any risk concerns upstream. Every school manager I know would rather have a staff member inform them about a possible or brewing situation ('It may be nothing, but. . .') than find out after a serious incident that someone on staff had some information about risk but hadn't shared it ('I didn't want to bother you. . . . I didn't think it would turn out to be anything.'). There are not likely to be major repercussions for escalating a situation that ends up not being particularly serious, but there could be serious repercussions for knowing about a situation of concern and *not* escalating it.

A few objections

The basic premise of this chapter (indeed, of this book) is that, if you see something of concern, do something about it. A simple conversation could save a life. Before we finish this chapter, however, I want to consider some common *objections* to the strategy that I am proposing here. Perhaps you've been wondering about these questions yourself over the recent pages.

Objection 1

'Really? You want me to talk one-on-one with every tricky kid in my class? Why can't I just give them a stern talking to or a detention? That should bring 'em into line!'

The idea expressed is that we can use the documented practices within our school's discipline policy to modify 'out of line' student behaviour. Such practices might include detentions, being kept back after class, time out for reflection or restorative practices. In extreme cases, schools may use suspensions or exclusions. My view is that these interventions have a place for students who are sufficiently skilled and stable to manage their own emotions and behaviour. By definition, however, the students I am concerned about are those who lack the skills or the stability to self-regulate, even with the threat of discipline. Remember that, in Chapter 2, we asked the question, 'How would I know if one of my students had an emotional or behavioural disorder?' Part of the answer was that the normal teacher interventions were failing to bring about the desired change. The conversations that I am proposing here may well only happen after the usual teacher interventions have not worked.

Objection 2

'Can't I just tell someone upstream in the school? Why do I have to speak directly to the student?'

This is a good question to ask. Starting by talking to an upstream colleague is a very reasonable option. Your upstream colleague may have some additional information that makes more sense of what you are observing in class and reassure you that the student is being well looked after. On the flipside, a direct conversation with a student, especially if you have some good pre-existing relationship, sends a message of care to your student. They may be more likely to open up directly to someone they know rather than have an upstream stranger investigate further. Your student may also feel some sense of betrayal that you didn't speak with them first. Which brings us to Objection 3. . .

Objection 3

'Won't telling someone upstream jeopardise my relationship with the student? Won't it betray their trust?'

Keep in mind that we only go upstream if we have information or suspicions that make us think there are genuine concerns (i.e. risk of harm or major educational implications) that need to be managed. Downstream school staff should never be left holding the responsibility for students with serious psychological disorders. It is perfectly reasonable to discuss your concerns with a colleague about what you are noticing in your class. In most situations, it is also possible to manage an upstream 'escalation' with respect and discretion such that the student need not feel betrayed about information they have personally shared with you.

On balance, this comes back to the principles we considered in Chapter 2 on managing the competing needs of respecting a student's privacy while also managing risk of serious harm. I would take this opportunity, though, to strongly advise that you never tell a student that you will keep information they tell you confidential, especially before you know what the information is that they are going to share. Some information just can't be kept confidential.

Objection 4

'You are kind of over-reacting here, aren't you? Most kids go through tough times but turn out just fine.'

It is true that many kids will go through tough times and then turn a corner to become happy and adjusted adults – often even without professional intervention. It is also true that many kids suffer silently for prolonged periods of time not knowing where or how to get help and never become happy or adjusted adults. I don't have a crystal ball to tell the difference between these groups. The best we can do is show these kids that they are not 'invisible' and that adults around them notice and care. My choice is to respectfully raise the concern with the student and see where it takes us rather than stay silent and hope things work out OK.

In a nutshell

- Conversations with students about emotional and behavioural concerns can be awkward, but when teachers notice concerns, they shouldn't just keep quiet.
- Find a convenient but quiet place to speak to a student of concerns – one that allows a degree of privacy but also that isn't too isolated.
- A simple 'formula' to take some of the difficulty away from the conversation is 'I've noticed that. . . . What's up?'
- Listen to the student's response to assess how serious their situation is. The worse the possible impact, and the more likely the scenario, the greater the risk.
- If you have concerns that a serious situation could be brewing, speak to a colleague 'upstream'.

Digging Deeper

1. For example, see Reinke, W. M. (2011). Supporting children's mental health in schools: Teacher perceptions of needs, roles, and barriers. *School Psychology Quarterly*, 26(1), 1–13; Graham, A., Phelps, R., Maddison, C., & Fitzgerald, R. (2011). Supporting children's mental health in schools: Teacher views. *Teachers and Teaching*, 17(4), 479–496.

2. In case you haven't already picked it up, I think Dr Greene's ideas are intelligently developed, respectful to students, and clearly articulated. Any of his books are worth digging deeper into, but if you are wondering where to start, I suggest his book *Lost and Found: Unlocking Collaboration and Compassion to Help Our Most Vulnerable, Misunderstood Students (and All the Rest)*. New York: John Wiley and Sons.

Classroom approaches to students with emotional and behavioural disorders

Eden

Eden Eastwood had been in Rohan's Year 11 Agricultural Science class all year. She was a quiet kid who usually sat up the back and kept to herself. She wasn't disruptive or rude but just a little on edge and 'vacant', like her mind was somewhere else. She hadn't always been so disconnected, but something seemed to have happened a few months ago. She stopped contributing to class discussions or asking questions. She did the bare minimum amount of work and seemed to be away from class a lot lately. Earlier in the year, he had tried to engage her with some of his school-famous goofy humour ('Who doesn't love a dad joke?'). Jokes and humour were a big part of Rohan's classroom banter, but when Eden didn't respond, he thought it best to just let her be. Rohan wasn't surprised when he received the email asking him to attend a lunch-time meeting of all Eden's teachers – he had suspected something wasn't quite right. The meeting was jointly run by the Year Adviser, Anna Crompton, and the Head of Learning Support, Lizzy Watkins. Anna told the meeting that Eden had been bullied by a group of girls since Year 8 but had not told anyone about it. This year, some particularly nasty things had been posted about her online, and her parents had discovered a journal in which she expressed suicidal thoughts. They had urgently taken her to the local adolescent mental health service, who diagnosed severe anxiety and depression and commenced psychotherapy and medication. Anna said Eden's parents had provided the school with a report

Classroom approaches

> from the psychologist making various recommendations about school management for Eden. At that point, Lizzy Watkins took over the meeting. She said that she had put together an individualised support plan that contained some instructions on how to teach Eden in light of her new diagnoses. They were expecting she might feel unwell while she adjusted to her new medicine. In particular, she said they would be making some adjustments to how Eden sat her upcoming exams. Rohan was very happy to do whatever was required. Lizzy also said that Eden and her parents had made a special request to clamp down on any classroom bullying. Rohan was thankful that bit didn't apply to his class. The jokes and humour that he and others in the class shared meant that all his students were relaxed. Lizzy said that there was a particular taunt that had highly offensive connotations for Eden and that no class teacher should tolerate: calling her 'Jade'. At that point, Rohan froze. He'd heard girls calling Eden 'Jade' numerous times over the year in his class. It sounded harmless to him, and the girls seemed to find humour in it. He had even called her 'Jade' himself earlier in the year, assuming it was her nickname. Immediately after the meeting, he did an internet search for the meaning of 'Jade' via an online urban dictionary. His heart sank.

As a clinical psychologist, the 'central thesis' of my professional life – and, indeed, of this book – is to prevent emotional and behavioural disorders from happening and to treat them if and when they do. If you are a teacher reading this book, however, you have a very different professional 'central thesis'. Your task is to educate young people with the skills and knowledge that will prepare them for responsible adult life. The point of common interest for the clinical psychologist and the teacher is in taking steps to ensure that students with emotional and behavioural disorders are functioning to the best of their ability at any given time in order to promote learning and development in the classroom, both for a student of concern and for the other students in the class.

The reality we face together, however, is that students with emotional and behavioural problems will bring specific challenges into the classroom every day, and these challenges will affect how they behave and how they learn. It is not sufficient, as we have done so far in this book, to develop some knowledge on how these disorders might present in the classroom and to have some skills for how to raise concerns and direct a young person to help. None of this helps with the central task of teachers in schools of providing a quality education for these and all students.

What can teachers do in the classroom that will help students with psychological disorders? That is the topic we are addressing in this chapter. Our focus will, necessarily, be general in nature. We won't be digging down into different classroom approaches for each of the disorders we've met so far. Rather, we will consider some broad themes on to how to manage and make accommodations for these students. If I could summarise the message of the most important thing that teachers can do for students with emotional and behavioural disorders, it would be this: run excellent classrooms.

Psychological needs in the classroom: same but different

Managing a classroom of diverse learners is something teachers are incredibly skilful at doing. We know that any group of 25 students will contain some with specific literacy or numeracy needs, some with specific sensory needs; others will bring cultural and linguistic considerations and/or different learning styles. We are well versed – or at least should be – in the reasons for and the requirements of disability legislation in the jurisdictions in which we work. We are well in the swing of accommodations for any and all of these students with unique learning needs. Managing emotional and behavioural disorders shouldn't be a challenge then, right?

When thinking about educating students with emotional and behavioural disorders compared to other diverse learners, we need to adopt an attitude of 'same but different'. The similarity comes from our familiarity with knowing we need to adjust our practice for the different learners in the classroom and that modifications and accommodations are all part of the normal teaching and assessment process. For various reasons, though, students with emotional and behavioural disorders will create specific challenges for our classrooms. For a start, we've already seen that many of these students won't be formally recognised and diagnosed. When we know *what* we are dealing with, we have power to adapt to it. If we don't know what we are dealing with, we are often left flying blind.

Second, educators have been thinking about how to manage traditional 'difficulties' – think here about dyslexia or deafness or even autism – for a long time, and the profession has a vast amount of accumulated knowledge

Classroom approaches

and skill in this area. By contrast, our thinking and skill base when it comes to managing students with anxiety disorders or trauma or eating disorders has not yet developed to the same level of sophistication.

Third, despite recent progress, there remains a good deal more misinformation and stigma associated with emotional and behavioural disorders compared to other learning and physical disorders. Students and their families may be far more reluctant to speak up or seek help or ask teachers to do anything that draws attention to psychological disorders. Similarly, there are still some 'old school' teachers who remain reluctant to see psychological disorders as being genuine or a reason to make adjustments in the classroom. Finally, the sheer volume of students with emotional and behavioural disorders in our classrooms now, in addition to those with other non-psychological needs, means that the mix and frequency of needs has become far more complex.

And so, what is the solution? What are the core elements of teaching students with psychological disorders in our classrooms? Let's zoom in for a closer look.

Teaching practices for students with mental disorders

We should all be familiar with the Positive Behavioural Interventions and Supports (PBIS) tiered framework. The PBIS pyramid reminds us that support for students can be conceptualised across three tiers: Tier 1 is aimed at supports and practices for *the vast majority* of students, Tier 2 looks at strategies and supports for targeting the 10–15% of students with some risks or specific concerns, and Tier 3 targets the few students (up to 5%) who require intensive and individualised supports to improve their learning outcomes. While all teachers are skilled at the Tier 1 universal supports for student success, students with emotional and behavioural disorders will fall under Tiers 2 and 3 in requiring additional support and consideration. The good news is that, to a very large extent, the key Tier 1 practices – the practices of good teaching for all students – remain very much the bedrock of teaching the Tier 2 and 3 students with emotional and behavioural disorders. The point of difference largely comes in the degree of individuality, intensity and collaboration in the implementation of these supports.

Classroom approaches

The engaging learning environment

Good pedagogy involves creating learning environments where students are *engaged and stimulated*. Okay, so that is probably the most self-evident and unnecessary sentence you will read all year, but it is one that is crucial to understand. Schools are not sports or social clubs or cafes or performing arts centres or counselling centres, even if all those things may happen at school. Core business is teaching and learning. The best thing any teacher can do for a student with an emotional–behavioural disorder is to run a stimulating and engaging classroom. These students need education to be stimulating and engaging *more than* their peers in order to counterbalance their hyperactivity, their low motivation, their distractibility, their diminished energy levels, or their constant worry and emotional pain and so on.

One student I have worked with, Jessie, found school attendance incredibly overwhelming due to social anxiety and low mood. A review of her attendance record, however, revealed that her attendance was surprisingly better on Wednesdays and Fridays. When I asked her about it, she explained, 'I have History on Wednesdays and Fridays. History class is too good to miss'. Something about this one class, and this one teacher, really connected with Jessie and was a key factor in getting her out of bed, out of the house and engaged in her learning.

What factors promote positive student engagement in school and learning? Of course, that is a question that goes to the heart of education and pedagogy and is central to teacher training. Without doubt, the best people to answer that question are the students themselves. This is not only my view but also that of the Commissioner for Children and Young People in Western Australia, who recently 'consulted' nearly 2000 school students from Year 3 to Year 12 on what *they* thought best supported student engagement.[1] The Commissioner's report divided their responses into two categories – the Primary Factors or 'Foundations' and the Secondary Factors or 'Accelerators'. Table 7.1 lists what students said, divided into these two factors. I suggest that you stop and consider each factor and ask how much they reflect your school, your classroom and your teaching practice.

I was especially struck by Finding 5 from the Commissioner's Report concerning what engagement looks like:

> The role of teachers in providing a stimulating and positive learning environment was, unsurprisingly, critical to students' school and

Classroom approaches

Table 7.1 Promoting Engagement in Learning

Primary Factors – The Foundations
Having friends and positive relationships with other students
Teachers who have a genuine interest in our wellbeing and future
Families who are involved and interested
Secondary Factors – The Accelerators
A positive, fair and supportive classroom environment
Teaching and learning that is interesting and relevant
Choices and a say on decisions that affect us
Feeling safe
Help to overcome personal issues
Feeling physically and mentally well

learning experiences. Schools offering a wide range of learning activities and demonstrating the relevance of the curriculum to students' life outside of school, and their future aspirations were seen as positively influencing engagement, particularly in the high school years. Importantly, practical, hands-on learning tasks and opportunities for physical activity were seen as highly positive by male and female students alike. In addition, when teachers were fair to all, had clear expectations and provided a safe and consistent learning environment, students stated they were more motivated and positive towards learning.

(p. 44)

The Western Australian Report was not an attempt to directly consider classroom approaches for students with emotional and behavioural disorders. And yet, if you want to know what you can do to help these students, my answer is simple: run good classrooms. Create classrooms that students *want* to go to. Whatever we do to make classrooms engaging and stimulating is beneficial for all students but especially helpful for those with emotional and behavioural challenges. There are, however, three specific areas of the engaging classroom that I want to highlight when we consider students with emotional and behavioural disorders: engaging classrooms are *relational*, engaging classrooms are *safe*, and engaging classrooms are *modified*. Let's look at these one at a time.

The relational learning environment

Good pedagogy involves creating learning environments where students are *known*. It is increasingly being recognised that the quality of the relationship between the teacher and the student is a strong predictor of a student's educational outcomes. Rather than a good teacher–student relationship being a chance event or related to the innate qualities of the teacher, it is known that relational proficiency in education is a pedagogical skill which can be learned and developed.[2]

While this relational pedagogy is an important factor for all students, it is particularly important for students with emotional and behavioural disorders. The reason for this is that these students are at greater risk of feeling disenfranchised and excluded at school and in the academic process. Sometimes, this stems from a student's disorder leading to increased absenteeism and/or presenteeism.[3] Sometimes, it stems from their disorder leading to impaired grades, which fuels academic disillusionment. Sometimes, it stems from these students receiving less praise and positive attention – or, worse, more criticism and negative attention – from teachers who don't understand the nature of their disorder. Whatever the reason, more than anyone, these students need teachers who know and understand them.

Young people with low self-esteem can easily convince themselves that nobody cares. School connectedness, including connectedness to teachers, is a key protective factor. When students feel 'known' by a caring teacher in a classroom, they are more likely to feel safe. Teachers who take a relational approach are far more likely to notice the small signs of distress at the earliest stages of concern – an untucked shirt in a usually neat kid, a rushed homework effort in a student who is usually careful, a chatty student becoming withdrawn, an easy-going kid becoming quickly annoyed. Relational teachers also use relationship to know and use each student's personal strengths and traits. This individual knowledge guides them in knowing when to clamp down quickly with a particular student but give some additional leeway to another; when to invite a student to answer a question in front of the class and when to allow a student to sit quietly; when to recognise that some submitted work is a 'personal best' for a struggling student, even if it is well below the class average; and so on.

There is no end to the ways in which teachers can build relationship with students. The most basic is simply knowing and using each student's name. Similarly, you can notice when a student is absent from class and follow up on their return with a question about their welfare: 'I missed you in class

Classroom approaches

yesterday, Ishaan – is all ok?' One conscientious teacher I know writes each of his students' birthdays into his diary at the start of the year and gives them a personal shout-out in class on their birthday. In fact, any comment that shows that you know a student as more than just a random face is a class can be pivotal. For example:

- I heard your mum is unwell, Beth. I hope she gets better soon.
- Mateo, I really like that haircut.
- Hey Johanna, I saw you get your award in Assembly yesterday. Great work!
- Ah, you've got your guitar here today, Joon. Are you learning some new songs?

The take-home point: Students with emotional and behavioural disorders need staff who work just that little bit harder to form relationships.

The safe learning environment

Good pedagogy involves creating learning environments where students are *safe*. Maslow reminds us that it isn't until students feel *safe* that they can pursue the higher-order goals, primarily 'self-actualising' through engagement and achievement in learning. It goes without saying that we want our students to feel both physically and emotionally safe at school. Feeling safe at school boosts school attendance, connection with peers and staff, connection with the learning process, academic achievement and overall personal development during the crucial formative school years.

Consider how safety may be particularly salient for students with psychological disorders. We can expect that students with anxiety disorders will routinely feel more on edge than their peers. Students who have been traumatised will be hypervigilant to further signs of threat, including inside the classroom. Students with ADHD will experience peer stigmatisation and rejection and accordingly be at risk of victimisation within the classroom.[4]

Notably, there are also some minority groups that we can expect to be feeling less safe in the classroom. LGBTQI students not only experience a lower level of safety at school due to discrimination based on their sexual orientation or gender identity but also are known to be at greater risk of psychological disorders. Likewise, refugee students who have come out of warzones or had other traumatic re-location experiences have the double risk of psychological disorders and a deep feeling of vulnerability. Even being from an ethnic minority within a school or community makes it more likely that you have experienced bullying or discrimination and therefore more likely that you will experience emotional distress. For all these groups, safety in the classroom becomes paramount.

Physical and emotional safety speaks directly to the culture of each classroom and to the school as a whole. My firm hope is that every teacher will take seriously their responsibility to establish a class culture of respect and safety. This begins with establishing clear rules from the very beginning of the academic year about what is, and what isn't, acceptable within the classroom. It then continues with the dual processes of noticing and praising students who uphold this culture and noticing and holding accountable those who undermine it. This is Class Management 101. It is within this culture that students with internalising disorders will more likely feel safe enough to relax and engage in their learning and that students with externalising disorders will more likely feel supervised and contained enough to manage their own behaviour.

Discipline in the classroom is essential. However, I'm not talking here about 'old school' discipline from the Dark Ages where a teacher might have threatened, intimidated or frightened their students into submission. Happily, this type of discipline is almost extinct now. Such discipline undermines relationship and safety. Rather, I'm talking about discipline where there are clear expectations and reasonable consequences for not meeting them.

Perhaps ironically, it is frequently students with emotional and behavioural disorders who will exhibit behaviours in class that require the most discipline. This will include the impulsive or hyperactive or oppositional students with externalising disorders. However, it will also include the internalising students who could be irritable or fail to complete work or who are tardy in their attendance and sloppy in their appearance. Conventional wisdom is that rules need to be applied in the same way and to the same standard for all students in the class. What's the point of having rules if they don't apply equally to everyone in the class, right?

The problem with this is that not all students have the same *capacity* to keep to the rules. One school in which I worked had bells to announce the end of each class followed by another bell five minutes later to announce the start of the next class. Five minutes was plenty of time for students to move between classes, and a standard rule was that students would receive a discipline if they made a habit of being late to class. While this rule was fair and achievable for most students, it was not achievable for Oliver, a student in a wheelchair who needed to navigate an indirect series of ramps and elevators to move between classrooms. There was no question that the rule needn't apply to him or at least needn't be applied in the same way for him.

Classroom approaches

Students with psychological 'disabilities' are no different to those with physical disabilities in terms of a school's need to have flexibility to accommodate for their disability. In this context, classroom discipline becomes more about applying the *spirit* of the law than the *letter* of the law. If we gave our hyperactive students a detention every time they called out in class or got out of their seat, they would have a detention every day of the week. We want to ensure that flexible school discipline is about creating safety for students without creating unhelpful apprehension for those with significant emotional or behavioural challenges.

The take-home point: Students with emotional and behavioural disorders need staff who work just that little bit harder to create a safe classroom.

The modified learning environment

Good pedagogy involves creating learning environments where students' individual learning needs are accommodated for. Almost always, students with emotional and behavioural needs are best served when they are attending school and learning in mainstream classes. Our job is to consider what types of adjustments we can make to allow them to attend, survive and engage in our classrooms. Schools are experienced at making adjustments for students with a broad range of disabilities. The good news is that many of the accommodations for students with learning or physical disabilities can be applied for students with emotional and behavioural disabilities. What may require some additional consideration, though, is knowing what types of modifications and accommodations are appropriate for students with emotional and behavioural disorders.

Classroom and assessment adjustments are best determined and disseminated in a coordinated fashion by those upstream rather than idiosyncratically invented by individual class teachers. This will most effectively be done in conjunction with the external mental health professionals, the families and the students themselves. If a classroom teacher is told that a student has been diagnosed with an emotional and behavioural disorder, it is very reasonable to ask those upstream what modifications the school will adopt to accommodate the student's needs. Individual Education Plans are just as necessary for students with emotional and behavioural disabilities as they are for those with learning or medical disabilities, just as state disability laws equally apply across any type of disability.

Table 7.2 provides a list of commonly applied classroom, instructional and assessment modifications that can equally be applied for students with

Table 7.2 Classroom Modifications for Students with Emotional and Behavioural Disorders

General Classroom Accommodations
Preferential seating within classroom
Permissions to move/stretch
Use of distress-tolerance aids (e.g., fidget toys, sensory aids)
Rest breaks within the classroom
Time out/permission to leave class to alternate supervised space
Altered school attendance schedule; late start or early finish
Designated 'Chill Zone'/calm space within the classroom
Establishing a peer buddy in the class
Permission to arrive or leave classroom a few minutes before others
Permission to eat/drink in class
Instructional Style Accommodations
More frequent reminders regarding appropriate behaviour (e.g. to stay on task, stay seated)
More frequent use of praise, encouragement and reward
Modified thresholds for when to implement discipline
Pre-arranged 'catch up' plan for classes student misses
Consideration of group composition (e.g. for two students who set one another off)
Additional help with scaffolding larger pieces of work
Alternate methods of content delivery (e.g. watch video rather than read chapter)
More/Less frequent feedback about progress
Pre-arranged system with student to cue upcoming questions in class
Checking for understanding of content
Provision of notes/summaries
Pre-emptively reviewing content for potentially 'triggering' material
Homework and Assignment Accommodations
Provide alternate assignment tasks if set task is unsuitable
Reduced expectation for volume of work produced
Adjustments to format of work (e.g. handwritten vs typed vs oral presentation)
Extended deadlines for assignments
Estimate some assessments based on other assessments
Exam Accommodations
Additional time
Rest breaks
Exam questions in an alternate format (e.g. essay vs multiple choice vs oral)
Separate/small group supervision
Alter time of examinations (e.g. schedule for later in day)
Reduced number of exams per day; one exam per day

emotional and behavioural disorders. The list is not exhaustive, and consideration must be given to which types of modifications will be most helpful for individual students.

The take-home point: Students with emotional and behavioural disorders need staff who work just that little bit harder to modify how the classroom and assessment process can accommodate them.

Engaging with students with emotional and behavioural disorders: two psychological approaches

So far in this chapter, we have looked at what we might consider *educational* approaches to accommodating students with emotional and behavioural difficulties. I now want to turn to two *psychological* approaches that can guide us with how we assist these students. In over three decades as a mental health professional, I've investigated just about every approach to promoting positive behaviour in young people that has been invented. I think there are two that warrant special merit for us as we seek ways to include and assist our students with emotional and behavioural disorders.

Strengths-based approaches

My profession of psychology has always had close links with the medical profession. The so-called 'medical model' is all about first diagnosing a problem so that you can then treat it correctly. Once you've diagnosed an infection, you can commence antibiotic treatment; once you've diagnosed cancer, you can begin chemotherapy or radiotherapy. We owe a great deal to the contribution of Sigmund Freud and his early attempts to understand, describe and treat emotional and behavioural problems. He was a medically trained physician who brought a medical model to the psyche: find the problem and devise a way to treat it. Over the 20th century, many subsequent models of understanding emotional and behavioural difficulties were developed, all of which had one thing in common: find the problem and treat it.

The latter part of the 20th century saw an important and radical development in the field of psychotherapy and our understanding of how to help those with emotional and behavioural disorders. I first became aware of this 'breakthrough' via the work of American family therapists Steve de Shazer and Insoo Kim Berg, who were the founders of Solution Focused Therapy. Rather than putting the focus on finding out about problems and their causes, they began to work with a focus on *solutions*. Rather than talking to their clients about all the things that had gone wrong in their past, they intentionally changed the focus to identifying the positive behaviours their clients wanted to have happen in their future. Rather than focusing on the factors that lead to problems, they began to focus on factors that lead to *exceptions* to those problems (that is, times when the problem wasn't apparent or wasn't as strong). And rather than focus on the deficits that existed in the life of their clients, they began to focus on the *skills and competencies* that their clients did have.

When I first encountered Solution Focused Therapy, I remember feeling that someone had drawn back the curtains and ushered in a whole fresh light on working with people who were experiencing difficulties. Consider the young person whose experience of life was characterised by trouble, disappointment, criticism and failure. They didn't want to come into a psychologist's office and be probed about how bad their life was. They felt hopeless enough as it was. Instead, by having a conversation about their hopes for the future, the skills that they already have, and the times (even if rare) when they experience success, we were able, even in small ways, to begin to instil some hope, self-belief and motivation for change. What powerful foundations for moving forward in a positive direction!

Since the pioneering work of de Shazer and Berg, we have seen a broadening of this type of approach from social work and psychology into management, coaching and education. This type of approach now falls within a broader umbrella that we can call a *strengths-based* approach. There is a whole field of strengths-based education you can explore. In fact, it fits very neatly with the Positive Education movement.[5] My hope is that a strengths-based approach may bring a new and refreshing perspective to how we manage students with psychological disorders in classrooms. In fact, it is these very students who are the ones most likely to make us feel hopeless and overwhelmed as educators. It is these students who are most likely to draw us towards a 'pathology' or 'deficit' approach, where we end up thinking, 'I can't get through to this student' or 'I need a psychologist to fix this student before I can teach them anything'. While it is true that

Classroom approaches

emotional and behavioural disorders may be an impediment to a student's learning, we don't want a second impediment to be that their teachers have put the student in the 'too hard' basket. And so, I encourage you to bring a new, strengths-based perspective to working with these students in your classroom. To this end, I offer three themes from this approach to guide your actions.

Looking for strengths

We are all 'good' at something. Sometimes, we are good at things *compared to other people.* You don't necessarily have to be an Olympian, but some people can just run faster, jump higher, play better or remember more than others. These are the ones at the far-right-hand end of the normal curve that we met in Chapter 2. More likely, however, is that we are just better at doing some things in our own life compared to other things in our life. Everyone has *relative* strengths and weaknesses, either compared to other people or compared to their other skills. Sometimes, these will be strengths that are evident within the classroom (such as being punctual or neat), and sometimes, they may be things that the student only does outside the classroom (such as skateboarding or playing trumpet). Sometimes, they will be directly applicable to the classroom (such as being persistent or organised) and sometimes, not directly so (such as being good at computer games or cooking). The strengths-based teacher is always on the lookout for things their students can do 'well'. And equipped with a knowledge of a student's strengths, an educator has powerful tools for teaching.

There are no rules for how you might use this knowledge, but let me throw a few ideas at you. Noticing a student's strengths and giving them a compliment will likely improve your relationship with that student ('I heard you have been chosen to be in the school musical, Matt – well done'). Noticing a student's strength will also build their confidence and motivation ('It looks like this calculus is coming more naturally for you than the geometry we did earlier in the year, Taylor').

Looking for exceptions

I've never met a kid who is 'bad' all the time. Sometimes, they are 'good' by the standards of other kids; sometimes, they are 'good' compared to what they are usually like. Either way, there will always be 'exceptions' when their behaviour is 'good'. The strengths-based teacher looks to notice these exceptions. They let the student know about the exception they've noticed. Bringing curiosity, they ask the student what has contributed to this example of change. There is power in changing the relational dynamic just by having a conversation about the occasional, exceptional outbreak of 'good', even if it is only a small or temporary outbreak. Importantly, asking about what has contributed to the exception can also lead to the discovery of things, even small things, that make a difference for good. This becomes an opportunity for a third strengths-based idea . . .

Amplifying small changes

Change happens in small steps. Using a strengths or solutions approach, we seek to take one small step at a time. When we notice exceptions or signs of even small change, we can then ask our student, 'What would it look like if things improved just one out of ten? What will you be doing when things have improved one out of ten? What might I (that is, you the teacher) be noticing when things are just one out of ten better?' There is an optimism and hope that comes with considering a better future. It is accompanied by a realistic belief in the possibility of change if the imagined step is achievably small – just a *one out of ten* step. In this way, we can help students achieve small, positive changes over time.

Collaborative and proactive solutions

The second approach to working in the classroom with students with emotional and behavioural disorders comes from the work of Dr Ross Greene, who we met earlier in this book. From the moment I started reading Dr Greene's work on CPS, it just made sense and resonated with everything that I had learned from working with young people in schools. Equally importantly, but perhaps not surprisingly, it came with body of evidence from university studies to support its efficacy.[6] Let me introduce you to just three core ideas behind CPS that every school staff member can incorporate into their practice.

'Kids do well if they can'

This is the simple yet powerful statement that underpins much of the CPS approach and that we met in Chapter 2. What kid wouldn't want to do well?

Classroom approaches

Given a choice of getting 30% or 90% in a test, every kid would prefer the 90%. Given a choice of having a teacher (or parent or anyone) praise them for a job well done or reprimand them for a job poorly done, every kid would prefer to receive the praise. And yet it is easy for teachers (or parents or anyone) to look at a student misbehaving and doubt that they actually want to do well.

To help explain this point, CPS offers the juxtaposed statement, 'Kids do well if they want to'. The concept of kids doing well only *if they want to* is understandable when a student can do the 'right' thing on occasions, but then not on other occasions. For example, a student might be able to pay attention or control her outbursts on enough occasions for teachers (or parents or anyone) to think, 'She can do it if she really wanted to – she just doesn't want to'. So, what is going on here, and how do we make sense of this?

The CPS model offers a no-nonsense response to this question: students don't do 'well' because they haven't yet developed the *skills* necessary to do so. CPS refers to this as 'lagging skills', and it becomes one of the central themes of the model. This is empowering for teachers. Teachers know about developing skills. We do it in schools every day. The CPS model directs us to think about what skills are lagging for the student and to consider how to upskill them. There are two other lessons we can take on board from the CPS approach as we consider teaching students with emotional and behavioural disorders, and the name gives it away. . . .

Collaboration

Students with emotional and behavioural problems, more than any other students, can leave a teacher feeling baffled, if not downright frustrated and annoyed by their behaviour. Many books have been written on classroom discipline and management practices. One great strength – and, compared to many other approaches, one great innovation – of the CPS approach is the emphasis on the teacher *collaborating* with others when working with students with difficulties. Teachers can collaborate with other teachers, Year Advisors, counsellors or parents. But there is one particularly vital collaborator in CPS: the students themselves. CPS teaches us that problem solving about difficult students is something that teachers do *with* the student rather that *to* the student. Dr Greene refers to the need for 'inside information' when trying to solve classroom problems, and the best person to provide

Classroom approaches

inside information is the student themselves. We have already seen in Chapter 6 that Dr Greene provides us with the simple first steps for how to do this – it's as simple as asking, 'What's up?'

Proactivity

For students displaying challenging behaviours in class, we have a choice between managing the behaviours in one of two ways: *reactively* or *proactively*. The *reactive* approach is to wait until the behaviour appears and then decide what to do. Unfortunately, the reactive choice has two major downfalls. First, you have to think fast, and your response can end up rushed and poorly thought through. Second, any rapid response runs the risk of being heavily tainted by teacher frustration, usually accompanied by a terse and abrupt manner and/or by language that can further enflame a situation. The alternative – and, not surprisingly, the approach advocated by the CPS model – is to be *proactive*.

Thankfully, most students with emotional and behavioural disorders will show a predictable pattern in their behaviours of concern. Sometimes, the observant teacher will be able to observe particular events that regularly trigger a behaviour of concern from a student. For example, I recall one teacher telling me she had noticed that a student with an autism spectrum disorder was much more likely to have meltdowns on windy days. Sometimes, such triggers cannot be available to teachers, either because the behaviours are caused by something unobservable (for example, a thought going through a student's mind) or because the trigger occurred outside the classroom (such as an interchange between students on the way to class). This is the argument for needing 'inside information'. In the context of a collaborative approach, the teacher and the student together can discuss the triggers and together and *proactively* plan a response for the next time they are 'triggered'.

In fact, the CPS approach says that the problematic behaviour that confronts the teacher (such as the class meltdowns of our student on windy days) is not actually the problem. Instead, the teacher needs to look at precipitating events upstream to better understand what skills the student hasn't yet developed to cope with some of their demands. When we work proactively – and collaboratively – we can anticipate difficulties, understand problems and develop solutions. When our teacher understood the role of windy days and the student's dislike of the feeling of wind on her skin, she also discovered that the student was better able to calm her distress through the tactile soothing of a small velvet pin cushion. An arrangement with the parents to keep a spare pin cushion in the classroom for windy days proved to be a proactive and productive prophylactic!

Perhaps you are left scratching your head with these ideas from CPS. 'Well, that's not very psychological – it just seems like common sense', you may be thinking. I 100% agree with you. And that is why I think it is so powerful.

Final thoughts

There is no better school-based help for students with emotional and behavioural disorders than running good classrooms. Thankfully, this is what teachers do best. A classroom environment that is engaging, stimulating and safe for all students is fantastic for students with emotional and behavioural concerns. It is also fair to say that these students will present teachers with some challenges that require special consideration above and beyond other students. Fortunately, there is a plethora of intelligent and wise people who have been putting their minds towards how to do this for many years, and we don't need to start from scratch or reinvent the wheel as we think about our own challenging students. I am not here to convert you to a particular approach for how to manage these students, but I do think there are some extremely valuable ideas that we can learn from them. The strengths-based and CPS approaches are two of the best. I have only scratched the surface of them in this brief chapter, but I do hope that I've whetted your appetite to find out more.

What you can do now, however, is start to think differently about students with challenging behaviours and draw on some helpful assumptions as you seek to make sense of their behaviours. As we start to *think* differently, we will start to *act* differently. Here are some concluding thoughts I'd love you to take back into your classrooms:

- All of my students have strengths; I just have to find out what they are.
- I can use my students' strengths to help them cope with adversity.
- Sometimes, the best way to focus on a problem is to figure out when the problem isn't there and make that happen more often.
- Students do well if they can, and if they can't, it is because they haven't developed the skills yet to do so.

Classroom approaches

- Problems are best solved collaboratively with my student.
- Problems are best solved proactively. I can anticipate difficulties and have a plan worked out in advance.

In a nutshell

- The best thing that any teacher can do for a student with an emotional and behavioural disorder is to run an engaging and stimulating classroom.
- Engaging and stimulating classrooms are characterised by being relational, safe and modified.
- The strengths-based approached to classroom management looks to notice and build on a student's strengths rather than their deficits. This includes noticing exceptions to 'the problem' and working with the student to amplify small changes.
- The Collaborative and Proactive Solutions approach to classroom management is based on the idea that kids do well if they can. School staff can proactively and collaboratively help students develop the lagging skills that prevent them from doing well.

Digging Deeper

1 This report makes for interesting reading and is available on the internet: Commissioner for Children and Young People. (2018). *Speaking out about school and learning: The views of WA children and young people on factors that support their engagement in school and learning.* https://www.ccyp.wa.gov.au/media/2763/speaking-out-about-school-and-learning.pdf

2 If you want to dive deeper into this, I suggest you read Hickey, A., Riddle, S., Robinson, J., Down, B., Hattam, R., & Wrench, A. (2022). Relational pedagogy and the policy failure of contemporary Australian schooling: Activist teaching and pedagogically driven reform. *Journal of Educational Administration and History*, 54(3), 291–305; Ljungblad, A. L. (2021). Pedagogical relational teachership (PeRT) – a multi-relational perspective. *International Journal of Inclusive Education*, 25(7), 860–876.

3 Are you familiar with the notion of presenteeism? It's the idea that a person can be physically present, for example at work or school, but not actually doing anything productive due to physical or mental illness or just having other pressing life 'stuff' that means that their head isn't 'in the game'.

4 This point is predicated on the reality that students with ADHD experience tangibly more peer victimisation and friendship difficulties than their peers without ADHD. You can dig deeper into that research here: Becker, S. P., Mehari, K. R., Langberg, J. M., & Evans, S. W. (2017). Rates of peer victimization in young adolescents with ADHD and associations with internalizing symptoms and self-esteem. *European Child and Adolescent Psychiatry*, 26(2), 201–214; Gardner, D. M., & Gerdes, A. C. (2015). A review of peer relationships and friendships in youth with ADHD. *Journal of Attention Disorders*, 19(10), 844–855; Mrug, S., Molina, B. S., Hoza, B., Gerdes, A. C., Hinshaw, S. P., Hechtman, L., & Arnold, L. E. (2012). Peer rejection and friendships in children with attention-deficit/hyperactivity disorder: Contributions to long-term outcomes. *Journal of Abnormal Child Psychology*, 40(6), 1013–1026.

5 If this intrigues you, you can explore further here: Lopez, S. J., & Louis, M. C. (2009). The principles of strengths-based education. *Journal of College and Character*, 10(4), 1–8; Galloway, R., Reynolds, B., & Williamson, J. (2020). Strengths-based teaching and learning approaches for children: Perceptions and practices. *Journal of Pedagogical Research*, 4(1), 31–45.

6 For a review of research on CPS, see Greene, R., & Winkler, J. (2019). Collaborative & proactive solutions (CPS): A review of research findings in families, schools, and treatment facilities. *Clinical Child and Family Psychology Review*, 22, 549–561.

Self-harming and suicidal students

Maisie

'What's that saying about herding cats?' thought Connie Li as she was mentally psyching herself up for her Year 8 Physical Education class. Today, she was starting a new topic on gymnastics. She was an experienced and capable teacher, but her position on the school's Work, Health and Safety Committee meant that she tended to overthink all the ways in which people could get injured. Some of her PE colleagues looked at the school's new trampolines, vaults and parallel bars with great excitement. Connie, on the other hand, looked at them and could only see falls, breaks, strains and concussions. Once her class had changed into their PE gear, she sat them all down on the floor of the gym for the mandatory safety lecture. To her surprise, today these 'herded cats' seemed to have channelled some 'sheep' qualities and were sitting almost quietly as she stood in front of them firmly stipulating the safety dos and don'ts on the use of the trampoline and vaults. A snigger and giggle from three girls sitting cross-legged at the front interrupted Connie's flow, provoking a stern and intense scowl at the girls. It was then that Connie noticed the marks on Maisie Macintyre's upper thigh. Connie tried not to stare, but in the moment, she found the sight quite alarming. She lost track of where she was in her safety lecture and needed a second to bring her attention back to the job at hand. On autopilot, she continued with her talk, but inside her head, she was processing what she had seen. Eight to ten symmetrical lines, each about 3 cm long. Maisie had sensed that Ms Li had seen her marks and immediately repositioned her hands into

> her lap. Over the course of the lesson, Connie tried, without success, to get another look Maisie's leg. She contemplated alternate hypotheses to her initial conclusion that these marks were self-inflicted, hoping that she might find a way to avoid having to take any further action. At the end of class, Maisie was quick to change back into her school uniform. Connie called her aside as the class was leaving. 'I noticed the cuts on your thigh today, Maisie. What's going on?' 'It's nothing to worry about, Miss', replied Maisie. 'I got scratched by my cat on the weekend'. 'Yeah, right', thought Connie.

Perhaps there is no more confronting topic for us to consider than suicide and young people. Those of us who have never experienced the desperation that leads to suicidal ideation may find it difficult to understand how a young person can arrive at such a place of anguish. For those of us who have experienced such desperation, reading this chapter may tap into our own deep hurt and suffering. I doubt that any of us of have escaped the pain, confusion, guilt, and futility associated with the suicide of a friend or family member. It is certainly the case that there is no subject that I would like to write about *less* than our topic in this chapter.

None of the emotional and behavioural disorders we have considered so far in this book present school personnel with the risk of imminent death. Students don't die of anxiety, depression or ADHD. Despite the frightening mortality risk of eating disorders that we learned about in Chapter 5, deaths from anorexia only happen following a period of extended illness during which families and health care professionals work together with a sufferer who has already been diagnosed. By contrast, working with a suicidal student really can be a genuine life-and-death matter. In the introduction to this book, I told the story of a student who was alive and apparently well one day and then dead the next. And so, for those of us who work in schools, it is imperative that we are prepared to respond in an informed, effective and compassionate way when we do encounter a suicidal student.

In this chapter, we consider the separate but related phenomena of self-harm and suicide in young people. First, we will look at an overview of how to recognise and make sense of self-harm followed by practical mental health first aid strategies for how to assist these students. We will then move on to students experiencing suicidal ideation, again looking at how to recognise, understand and provide first aid for these students.

Making sense of self-harm

Let's begin this discussion by getting a few things straight. The first relates to the unhelpful use of differing expressions to describe what is, for our purposes, essentially the same thing. In the mental health literature, you will discover various names for self-harm, such as deliberate self-harm, non-suicidal self-injury, self-mutilation and self-injurious behaviour. In this book, I'll use the simple expression 'self-harm' to encapsulate all these terms – let's move on and not get distracted by terminology.[1]

Second, most young people who self-harm don't do so with any intention to take their own life. Self-harm isn't a mini or unsuccessful suicide attempt. So, how should we make sense of self-harm in young people? Perhaps the best answers to this question are provided in a study completed by Dr Donna Gillies and an international team of collaborators from Greece, Canada, Mexico and the United Kingdom.[2] They carried out a meta-analysis in which they reviewed all studies on adolescent self-harm between 1990 and 2015 to better understand its prevalence and characteristics. They reported that, across all the studies reviewed, the lifetime prevalence of self-harm in adolescents was 16.9% with higher rates in girls than boys. Disturbingly, the average age at which young people first self-harm is 13 years. The reason most commonly cited by adolescents for self-harming, and one that resonates strongly with my clinical experience, was 'to obtain relief from feelings or thoughts'. Other reasons cited were summarised as 'to punish oneself', 'to let someone know or get a reaction' and 'to feel something even if it was pain'. Young people may not use these exact words, but these sentiments will account for almost all self-harm in young people.

For our purposes, the reasons young people give for self-harming are not the most important thing we need to know. More valuable is to know *what to look out for* as signs of self-harm. In fact, the number of ways that young people have found to hurt themselves is innumerable, and a genuinely distressed person can find ways to self-harm wherever they are, using whatever they have. That said, it is certainly the case that there are some more commonly used methods, and the Gillies meta-analysis gives us some guidance here on what to look for. Self-cutting was (and is) by far the most commonly used method of self-harm. While students can cut anywhere on the body, the most frequent locations include the arms, wrists, thighs or stomach. Other forms of self-harm reported by Gillies and her team included preventing wounds from healing (for example, picking at scabs), head banging, biting, scratching, hitting, self-poisoning/overdose and burning. The take-home message for school staff is to be on the lookout for *any* signs of unusual injury.

Although I've said that self-harm is usually not an intention to take one's life, it is a mistake to then think that we don't need to take self-harm seriously. In fact, quite the opposite is true. Self-harm is a sign that a young person is experiencing serious emotional distress for which they don't have more functional or effective coping strategies. Moreover, self-harm frequently occurs comorbidly with a range of other emotional and behavioural disorders, including depression, eating disorders, trauma and BPD.

There is one other menacing comorbidity with self-harm: suicidality. While the act of self-harming isn't intended to end one's life, it is often found in young people who are having such thoughts. Accordingly, we must never downplay the significance of self-harm within a student's broader emotional health. It is no exaggeration to say that the school staff member who notices and responds to signs of self-harm could genuinely be the catalyst in saving the life of a suicidal young person.

Responding to the self-harming student

We move now from the theory to the practice of self-harm: what can we do when confronted with a student who has self-harmed? Sometimes – though, in my experience, not often – a student may initiate directly telling a staff member that they have been purposefully hurting themselves. More likely is that we notice some unusual marks on a student's body that raise suspicions, such as with our vignette of Maisey, or that concerned peers may approach a teacher to report the activity of one of their friends. Regardless, when we receive information of a student self-harming, the one thing we *can't* do is ignore it. It may be that a downstream teacher decides to escalate the information to someone upstream. I would like to outline here a three-point plan of attack for the staff member – whether upstream or downstream – who needs to talk to a self-harming student. The plan involves our *attitude*, our *assessment* and our *action*. We'll consider these one at a time.

Our attitude

Winston Churchill is reported to have said, 'Attitude is a little thing that makes a big difference'. This is certainly the case when we are responding to students who have self-harmed and, even more so, to students who have expressed suicidal thoughts. Our attitude becomes the base of the pyramid on which all our other responses rest. Take a moment to consider the 'headspace' of these students, especially those students who are revealing their self-harm secret for the first time. Almost inevitably, they feel out of control, helpless, hopeless, most likely ashamed or guilty or afraid, or all these things combined. Frequently, they feel let down or blamed or wronged by significant adults in their life. Even from a young age, children sense the taboo and stigma that surrounds self-harm and suicide. And now, an adult, perhaps one they hardly know, is aware of their secret. 'How is this adult going to react?' they will wonder.

And how will you react? *Shock* is a normal reaction to information that is literally shocking. Or we may feel *frightened* by our own inadequacy to deal with this level of distress. Or perhaps *irritated* because we had other plans for this hour, which now need to be changed on short notice. More than irritated, we may feel downright *angry* that someone would think that to hurt themself or, worse, to kill themself is in any way a sensible response to life's challenges. Needless to say, none of these represents the attitude that is going to help our distressed young person.

And so, when we are confronted with our distressed student, our attitude must be characterised by calmness rather than calamity and compassion rather than criticism. Calmness involves the ability to override those initial negative responses sufficiently that your student can see that you are not shocked or afraid or overawed by the news you have received. Sometimes, this requires the mental reminder to breathe slowly even as you can feel the adrenaline pumping through your veins and your heart rate soaring. Sometimes, it requires the self-control to stay still and quiet even as your mind is screaming, 'Do something'. The student must be able to watch your reaction and conclude, 'I haven't freaked her out'.

Compassion is that response of the heart that says, 'I care, and I'll do all I can to support you'. It is the response that sees the student's distress and, with empathy and kindness, wants to help. For some of us, this response of calm and compassion can come reasonably naturally. For others of us, when confronted by a situation that is well outside our comfort zone, calm and compassion are far from our default attitude. What I can say is that, the more often you respond to these situations, the better you become at tapping into the desired attitude. Until that happens, it is often just a matter of 'fake it 'til you make it'.

Regardless of what the student sees in your response, there are some words that you can say which will help ensure that the right attitude is conveyed:

'I'm so glad you had the courage to tell me/show me this.'

'I want you to know that I care for you and will do all I can to help make things better.'

Our assessment

Our assessment of the self-harming student must cover two areas: the emotional health risk and the physical health risk. Assessment of the emotional health risk is reasonably straightforward. Any student who has self-harmed must be considered to be emotionally 'at risk', and, accordingly, action must be taken. It is as simple as that. We'll look at the action shortly.

Assessment of the physical risk, however, is a little more complex. Sometimes, the physical harm can be very minimal and present very minor physical risk. A common presentation in schools, for example, is a student who has made superficial scratches on their skin which might require only minor first aid. At the other end of the spectrum is the student who has reported self-poisoning or taking an overdose, which presents a substantial health risk and could be life threatening. The overriding principle here is that the physical component of the self-harm needs to be assessed and treated according to the usual practices of *physical* first aid.

Such assessment will require some information gathering. It is perfectly reasonable to ask the student to describe what they have done to themselves and to follow up with some clarifying questions so that you can better assess the risk they face from their harm. Clarify questions could include further details on how they have hurt themselves; a description of their wound(s), such as the location, length, depth or number; how recently they have self-harmed; and what, if any, first aid they have already applied. It is also reasonable to ask the student if they would be willing to show you any wounds they have inflicted. They may decline, and we should respect that decision, or they may be prepared to show you. The obvious limitations around this are that a student, like any person receiving first aid, should never be touched without their permission, and it is not appropriate to ask a student to reveal private body parts (for example, inner thigh, breasts, buttocks) for the purposes of assessing self-harm. Based on the information we are told, or shown, regarding the self-harm, we can make an assessment of the extent of the physical injury using standard first aid practises.

Our actions

Our action on discovering that a student has self-harmed will now be guided by our assessment. In relation to physical risk, our action is the application of appropriate physical first aid. Sometimes, no immediate physical first aid is required – for example, if the student has only minor bruising. At other times, there may be a need for bandaging or application of antiseptics. The most concerning risk is with students who have just ingested poisons or purposefully overdosed. This scenario could be life threatening, and emergency treatment or an ambulance will be needed. It is beyond the purposes of this book to detail the practices of physical first aid other than to endorse the importance of all school staff having up-to-date first aid training. Schools that have a nurse on site can also take the student to the school clinic for more professional assessment and treatment.

Regarding the actions for the emotional health risk, any student who is self-harming requires referral to a mental health professional for further assessment of their mental state. Accordingly, no school personnel should keep a secret about a student's self-harm. For the downstream school staff, managing such a referral will usually require sharing information upstream. For the upstream school staff, managing the referral will usually involve informing parents and helping facilitate a referral to a community-based mental health professional. Schools with a psychologist or mental health social worker on staff can use the expertise of the in-school professionals to guide this process.

Of course, it would be naïve to think that self-harming students will be happy for you to share their 'secret', and we should expect some resistance to you telling other people about the self-harm. Consider our vignette of Maisie, whose first response when approached by her teacher was to fabricate a story that she hoped might be sufficient to throw the teacher off track. Nonetheless, the risks of serious injury with self-harming or suicidal students are too important to ignore. There remains one further important question to consider when speaking with a self-harming student: could they also be having suicidal thoughts?

Self-harming and suicidal students

Responding to the suicidal student

The frightening reality is that it is not uncommon for young people to experience suicidal thoughts or take suicidal actions. The most comprehensive investigation of suicidality in young people to date is by Anna Van Meter at the Department of Child and Adolescent Psychiatry at New York University.[3] Dr Van Meter and her team carried out a meta-analysis of every study of suicidal ideation or suicidal attempts in youth published between 1981 and 2021. They found that the weighted average prevalence rates across these studies was 16.4% for suicidal ideation, 9% for suicidal ideation with a plan, and 6.2% for suicide attempts. The point we can take from this is that suicidal ideation and suicide attempts are not uncommon in our school communities, even if we don't know or hear about many of them. As you would expect, prevalence rates varied depending on many factors with higher rates in older students than younger and in girls compared to boys. We also know from many other studies that LGBTQI youth have much higher likelihood of experiencing suicidal ideation, as do any students with any other mental health diagnosis.

And, as I hope you've learned by now, it is not uncommonly school staff who are the first to see signs of mental distress, even before a student's parents or a mental health professional. Sometimes, hints of suicidal thoughts come out in caring conversations between students and a trusted school staff member, including during a conversation about self-harm. Sometimes, a student will reveal suicidal themes in their schoolwork. I've seen this on many occasions: the English student whose creative writing revolves around a suicide, the Fine Art student whose paintings depict despair and suicide, or the Drama student writing a soliloquy about a hopeless person considering ending a meaningless life. I've even seen a Science student reveal suicidal ideation during a unit on forensic science. Of itself, a student choosing to have suicidal representations in their work doesn't mean they are suicidal, but it does raise questions that the insightful teacher must consider. It becomes one piece of a broader puzzle – a piece that the staff members should escalate so that those upstream can seek to assemble all the available pieces.

Once again, our response to the student with suicidal thoughts can be considered within the categories of our attitude, our assessment and our actions. If our attitude was important for self-harming, it is even more so when we think of students who are expressing suicidal thoughts. We will

Self-harming and suicidal students

focus here on the specifics of our assessment and our actions in the event of students revealing suicidal thoughts.

Our assessment

Let's begin by again stating our intention that school staff are not mental health professionals and should not be responsible for assessing a student's suicide status. Our role is to determine whether there are concerns of risk and, if so, to facilitate referral to someone better qualified to make a comprehensive assessment. To do this, though, requires school staff to be educated enough to notice warning signs and informed enough to make a call on *broad* risk. That is all we are trying to do here. Mental health professionals view suicide risk through levels of concern. Our purpose in outlining these here is so that, as you talk with students, you can seek to slot the information you have into broad risk categories.

Thoughts, but no intention

The first level of concern relates to student who have thoughts of being dead, without any genuine intention to act on those thoughts. This is the student who feels so overwhelmed by their current circumstances that they think, 'It would be better for me if I had never been born/wasn't alive anymore'. It is the reaction of feeling hopeless and wanting to be free of the current distress but with *no intention or plan to act on these thoughts*. Students at this level say things like, 'I think about it, but I would never do it'.

Making plans

The next level of risk relates to students who not only wish they weren't alive but are actually having *thoughts about how to bring their wish about*. Risk levels rise considerably for these students. The two key indicators to listen for are whether these students have made a plan for *how* they might end their life and for *when* they might end their life. Even a student who reveals that they possess a sophisticated knowledge of suicidal methods raises a red flag regarding why they have such knowledge. Risk level rises significantly if they reveal a 'how' and 'when'.

Access to means

Risk level rises yet again if the student has *access to means to carry out their plan*. It is not aways the case that a student has such means – for example, a student who makes a plan to shoot themselves but doesn't have access to a gun. Frequently, however, students will make a plan based on what they know they have access to. Great concern is triggered for the student who has already procured or has easy access to their chosen means.

Previous attempts

The strongest predictor of suicide is whether a person has made a previous suicide attempt. School staff should therefore take very seriously any student who makes known they have previously made an attempt on their own life – either recently or in the past. It is grave mistake to disregard such actions by thinking 'It's just attention seeking' or, worse, 'If they really meant to do it, they would have done it properly'.

These four 'levels' of risk become an assessment framework into which school personnel can slot the 'incidental' information they have become aware of. By 'incidental', I am referring to information that comes to a staff member without any specific investigation or probing. No single piece of information alone is sufficient to fully assess risk. Any suicide-specific information a staff member receives can be integrated with the broader picture they have from their knowledge of the student. Importantly, lack of information does not provide any reassurance of a student's risk status. That is, just because a student didn't say that they have made a plan doesn't mean that they haven't made a plan.

Some staff may feel competent and confident enough to supplement incidental information by asking some clarifying questions to better understand the circumstances of the student of concern. These questions may not be appropriate for all staff to ask, but they certainly help tease out levels of risk. Again, attitude underpins the success of such questions. It is about curiosity conveyed with calmness and compassion. Each level of risk can be explored through a single question with the answer to each question determining whether asking about the next level is required.

Level 1: Have you ever had thoughts about taking your own life?

Level 2: Have you considered how you would do it? Have you considered when you would do it?

Level 3: Do you have access to (the means for the revealed method)?

Level 4: Have you previously tried to take your life?

Our action

Our action is again determined by our assessment. As with physical first aid, the actions themselves are not complex, but they do require courage and commitment. Put simply, the school's actions for any student with suicidal thoughts is to facilitate steps towards professional assessment and treatment. Again, this is usually the action of an upstream member of the school community. The responsibility of the downstream school member is to bring the information to the attention of the relevant upstream staff. However, for students experiencing suicidal thoughts, the stakes are considerably higher than for those showing early signs of emotional–behavioural disorders or even for those who are self-harming. There is a level of urgency and risk that does not allow for a margin of error. Schools are advised to adopt the cautious approach that a student expressing suicidal ideation is a genuine risk to themselves. Moreover, we should continue to hold that view until a more comprehensive assessment from a mental health practitioner has been made. Accordingly, information that a student is experiencing suicidal ideation should be acted on immediately.

Any student who has revealed new information to a school staff member that they have made a plan about when or how they might take their own life – even if that plan is 'not now and not here' – should not be left unattended. Rather, they should be supervised until a parent or guardian can collect them and organise a mental health assessment. It then becomes a matter for the parent/guardian and a community-based professional to comprehensively assess risk and formulate an intervention plan. Even if a student is having suicidal ideation without a plan to act, this information should be given to the parents/guardians, and the school should expect a professional assessment and guidance from the external practitioner.

Final thoughts

Self-harming and suicidal students are clearly of the greatest importance for schools, and, in this brief chapter, we can only provide fundamental information within the realms of mental health literacy and first aid. Before we conclude this chapter, however, there are several final comments that need to be made.

School policy on suicidal and self-harming students

Students who are self-harming or suicidal are the most vulnerable and at-risk of all students within a school. Management of these students should not be left to chance or hastily cobbled together in the heat of a crisis. Rather, schools should have a *pre-determined* plan that guides all staff on how to respond in the event of concerns about self-harm or suicide. It is the responsibility of upstream staff to ensure that the school has clear guidelines to direct staff in the event of receiving information that raises any concerns. Moreover, it is the responsibility of upstream staff to ensure that such a policy is adequately communicated to the broader staff. It is the responsibility of downstream staff know the content of such a policy in sufficient detail to be able to act when required. Like all school policies, such a document will provide well-considered action during an emergency and the protections for staff members that come from closely following school policies and procedures.[4]

The value of a suicide risk assessment

Much of a school's management of suicidal students is based on the risk assessment provided by a suitably qualified mental health professional. The point must be made, however, that risk assessment is a very imprecise science. A student's risk status can change in an instant with the receipt of one text containing unwanted news, reading one unkind online post, getting a disappointing exam result, or the number of drinks consumed at a party. Schools should value the opinion and assessment of the external professional but continue to be vigilant regarding changes in the student's mental health status.

Balancing the risk to the individual student and the broader student body

School management must always be balancing the needs of the individual student against the wellbeing of the broader school community. In this chapter, we have focussed on what can be done to care for the self-harming and suicidal student. Also important is to consider the effect of these students on the broader student body. To witness another student self-harming or, worse, in the act of suicide is highly distressing for others within the school community – students and staff alike. A colleague of mine shared her story

Self-harming and suicidal students

of trauma when she had been called to identify the body of a student who had taken his life during the school day in the school bathroom. Moreover, the contagion effects of suicide and self-harm are real and have been well described.[5] Situations like this pose a potential risk for the entire community that school management must be cognisant of.

Return to school plan

I have made the point that self-harming and suicidal students need immediate professional assessment and an ensuing management plan. There are two critical implications of this. Firstly, schools need to liaise with external mental health providers to be clear about the nature of the ongoing risk and how the school can mitigate this risk. Secondly, self-harming and/or suicidal students should not return to school until there is a clear plan on how to manage the student's wellbeing and any ongoing identified risk. Ideally, such a plan should be developed and agreed on by the school, the parents, the external providers and, most importantly, the student themselves.

In a nutshell

- Self-harm is a common response by young people who are experience strong distressing emotions but who don't have more effective coping skills to manage their distress.
- The most common form of self-harm is cutting, but other methods include burning, scratching, biting, head-banging and self-poisoning.
- Students who self-harm often have a genuine emotional disorder, such as depression, an eating disorder, borderline personality disorder or substance abuse.
- Responding to self-harming students requires school staff to attend to both the physical first aid and the mental health first aid.
- Self-harming doesn't necessarily mean that a student is having suicidal ideation, but it is a risk factor for suicidal ideation.
- Teachers may be the first people to get hints that a student is having suicidal thoughts. Sometimes, this is through conversations with the student, or sometimes, it is expressed in their schoolwork.

Self-harming and suicidal students

- Any suicidal thoughts are concerning, but the level of risk increases if
  - the student has a plan for when or how they would take their life,
  - the student has the means to implement their plan, and
  - the student has made previous suicide attempts.
- A suicidal student should not be left unattended. Rather, they should immediately be transferred to the care of their parent/guardian and receive a comprehensive mental health assessment.

Digging Deeper

1 OK, I know I said 'let's move on' with definitions, but there is one thing I'd like to get straight. Sometimes, a young person's self-harm occurs in the action of an attempt to end their life. This is where the differing definitions come in. If there is no intention of suicide, it is usually referred to as 'non-suicidal self-injury'. If a mental health professional or researcher is seeking to use a word to capture self-harm that happens both with and without suicidal intent, they may use the broader term 'deliberate self-harm'.

2 Gillies, D., Christou, M. A., Dixon, A. C., Featherston, O. J., Rapti, I., Garcia-Anguita, A., Villasis-Keever, M., Reebye, P., Christou, E., Al Kabir, N., & Christou, P. A. (2018). Prevalence and characteristics of self-harm in adolescents: Meta-analyses of community-based studies 1990–2015. *Journal of the American Academy of Child and Adolescent Psychiatry*, 57(10), 733–741.

3 Van Meter, A. R., Knowles, E. A., & Mintz, E. H. (2023). Systematic review and meta-analysis: International prevalence of suicidal ideation and attempt in youth. *Journal of the American Academy of Child and Adolescent Psychiatry*, 62(9), 973–986.

4 For those wanting to dig deeper into school policies for self-harm and suicidal behaviour, I suggest Emily Berger and Janis Whitlock's Chapter 'Self-Injury response and intervention policy' in Allen, K.-A., Reupert, A., & Oades, L. E. (2021). *Building better schools with evidence-based policy: Adaptable policy for teachers and school leaders* (1st ed.). London: Routledge; Coen, J. (2016). *School safety and the duty of care: Managing students with serious mental health issues in mainstream schools*. Sydney: Kidscounsellor.com.au.

5 Young people are particularly vulnerable to social contagion, in part due to the importance of peer influence at this stage of their development, coupled with their extensive use of social media. This is a complex area, but you can dive in

further here: Martínez, V., Jiménez-Molina, Á., & Gerber, M. M. (2023). Social contagion, violence, and suicide among adolescents. *Current Opinion in Psychiatry*, 36(3), 237–242; Vidal, C., Lhaksampa, T., Miller, L., & Platt, R. (2020). Social media use and depression in adolescents: A scoping review. *International Review of Psychiatry*, 32(3), 235–253; Swedo, E. A., Beauregard, J. L., de Fijter, S., Werhan, L., Norris, K., Montgomery, M. P., Rose, E. B., David-Ferdon, C., Massetti, G. M., Hillis, S. D., & Sumner, S. A. (2021). Associations between social media and suicidal behaviors during a youth suicide cluster in Ohio. *Journal of Adolescent Health*, 68(2), 308–316.

Getting help

Charlotte – Part 1

Bec Fineman was having 'one of those days'. It was the day she was timetabled to teach every lesson bar one. How does that happen? Surely the School Executive could wrangle something so that Year Advisors like Bec had a greater time allowance to manage all the other challenges of her Year 10 cohort. Bec was very organised and had planned her 'to do' list for what she thought was achievable in her 50 minutes of 'free' time.

  TO DO

- Send email to parents about Year 10 Work Experience
- Follow up Billy Jesamine's excuse for not attending after-school detention
- Mark Year 7 progress tests
- Review end-of-term exam timetable
- Call Viraj Kumar's mum to find out how Viraj's chemo treatment is going
- Eat lunch

Sure, it was ambitious for one hour, but Bec lived on hope and coffee. Just as she began typing her parent email, there was a knock on the door. She looked up to see Amber Jamison, the Drama teacher. 'Can I have a minute?' she asked. Bec knew that 'a minute' never actually took a minute. Amber proceeded to tell Bec that, during Year 10 Drama class today, she had noticed a series of symmetrical cuts on Charlotte Bonucci's left arm. Bec was alarmed but not entirely surprised.

> Although she hadn't had much to do with Charlotte, over the past few months she had noticed Charlotte had been somewhat withdrawn and perhaps a little more sullen than usual. Something was 'brewing'. Bec picked up the phone to call in their school counsellor to help plan a response and then remembered that their part-time counsellor didn't work on Fridays. 'What use is a counsellor who isn't available when you need them?' thought Bec. She knew she couldn't ignore Amber's revelation, particularly with the weekend approaching. She needed to know if Charlotte was in any way a risk to herself and to make sure she got properly assessed. She immediately informed her Deputy Principal that she needed a replacement for last period and then got Charlotte out of class. Bec told Charlotte that Mrs Jamison had noticed the cuts on her arm – and indeed, Bec could see evidence of the cuts under the sleeve of her jumper. In the conversation that followed, Charlotte revealed to Bec that she had been cutting for a few weeks; that there had been significant tensions at home for over a year; and that her mum and dad had a major fight about two weeks ago, after which dad moved out, and she didn't know where he was. Bec knew from her Mental Health First Aid training that Charlotte was also at risk of having suicidal thoughts. To be honest, that wasn't a conversation she wanted to have. However, with the weekend just an hour off, and without the backup of the school counsellor, she knew what she had to do. Collecting as much calm as she could, and fearing the response she would get, Bec asked Charlotte, 'Have you had thoughts of ending your own life?'

Introduction

All good novels and movies take their audience on a journey towards a climactic conclusion. For us, everything we have done so far in this book has just been the groundwork for this *climactic* chapter. We have considered how we can tell the difference between 'normal' and 'concerning' behaviour. We have learned about the common types of emotional and behavioural disorders that young people experience. We have been through the steps to opening up a conversation with a student. But what next? What is the climax to the story once we know that we have formed the view that a student is genuinely in need?

The anti-climactic climax

One test of the quality of a TV show is its longevity. Many shows get a brief run, might develop some 'buzz'; many even get a second or third series but then fall into a pit of obscurity. Not so the 1970s American TV series M*A*S*H. I loved watching M*A*S*H as a kid and to this day can still find it playing on free-to-air TV here in Australia. This show has that rare ability to make the viewer laugh and cry all within the space of a 25-minute episode. It is no wonder the show ran for 11 seasons.

In one memorable episode, Company Clerk 'Radar' O'Reilly and the Chaplain, Father Mulcahy, are transporting a patient in a jeep through the remote Korean countryside when, suddenly, bombs begin exploding around them. Their patient begins choking and stops breathing. Radar and Father Mulcahy pull over to provide first aid. In desperation, they radio back to the hospital base seeking emergency guidance from the doctors. Up steps Alan Alda's character, Dr Hawkeye Peirce, who gives Father Mulcahy instruction over the two-way radio on how to perform an emergency tracheostomy on the back seat of the jeep using nothing but a pocketknife and an eyedropper tube, all the while with bombs continuing to explode around them. The tension builds, the soldier's life is in the balance, the 'operation' is a success, the good guys win, and they all live happily ever after. I LOVED it!

If this is the type of climax you are seeking for this first aid 'novel', I'm afraid that you are going to be deeply disappointed! The climax to this book may well be life changing for the young people involved – and for you, depending on the nature of the situations that you encounter – but ultimately, it should be neither dramatic nor climactic. And, as an additional twist, our conclusion is definitely *not* rocket science and is definitely *not* difficult. So, here it is, the climax to this book (cue swelling orchestral music please): schools need to link up students of concern with available mental health services in their local community. That's it. No emergency tracheostomies, no open-heart surgery and not even any talking people down from a rooftop. Our job in schools is simply to facilitate getting those students who need extra care to extra care.

Pathways to care

For mental health professionals, this pathway of getting at-risk young people connected to suitable care in the community is so vital that we've thought up a name to describe the process: *pathways to care*! OK, so we're not an imaginative lot, we mental health professionals, but the concept is straightforward – we want to get the right 'patients' to the right services as quickly as possible.

Consider the scenario of people with cardiovascular disease, cancer, infection, diabetes or just about any condition you can think of. It is well established that the health outcomes for these people are greatly maximised to the degree that they receive appropriate treatment from the suitable specialist at the earliest possible time. The principle is exactly the same for mental illness. In Chapter 2, we learnt the sobering statistic that about half of young people with a diagnosable mental disorder are not receiving any treatment and that there is frequently a significant time lag between the initial onset of symptoms and the time that a person actually gets help. Make no mistake about this: just as for physical health conditions, a failure to get timely and appropriate help for emotional and behavioural disorders reduces the likelihood of favourable outcomes for our students. Streamlined pathways to care are not just a quaint idea dreamed up by researchers with too much time on their hands. It may well mean the difference between life and death for those students we are responsible for.

Whose job is what?

At this point, we need to stop and ask a question: in schools, who is responsible for the process of the pathway to care? Whose job is it to refer students to external community-based help? These pathways to care require explicit and streamlined coordination, and the process can't be ad hoc. This process requires a good deal of knowledge and care and accordingly sits firmly as a responsibility of the upstream members of the school community rather than the downstream staff. The role of those downstream is to escalate their concerns upstream, while those upstream will have the responsibility of managing the process from school to community-based service.

The next question is the obvious objection: isn't it the parents' job to get help for their children? Clearly, the answer to this question is a resounding 'yes'. Best pathways to care models are those where, whenever and wherever possible, schools transfer the responsibility for a student getting appropriate help to the student's parents or guardians. In fact, it is usually not the case that a school staff member can directly refer a young person to community-based mental health services. That step must be made either by the student themselves or in concert with their parents or guardians. Moreover, parents can and should provide a broad range of assistance to their children that schools simply cannot provide. This includes legal authority to consent to treatment with younger students. At a more practical level, it includes the process of transporting their child to the community service and, if relevant, paying for such a service.

At a therapeutic level, the help of parents is usually vital in helping the student cope better with their emotional and behavioural distress. Sometimes, this involves parents, at the direction of a clinician, changing their own behaviours which could be contributing to the student's difficulties. Sometimes, this involves parents learning strategies to help students manage their distress. Regardless, whenever possible, parents must be the main conduit for a young person receiving mental health assistance in the community.

So, what is the role of the school in this situation? I believe that schools can play two key roles in this process. First and foremost, this must involve the school informing the family of any emotional and behavioural concerns they have for the student if there is a risk of harm for the student. As a parallel, schools wouldn't think twice about informing parents about a student experiencing a serious *physical* concern while at school. Consider here the student who has suffered a broken leg or had an epileptic seizure while at school. The second process in which schools can involve parents is by offering some guidance about the types of mental health services available within their local community. Many parents navigating the world of mental health services for the first time have very little idea about where to start. By contrast, school wellbeing systems will likely have regular connection with local doctors, counsellors and clinics. Although it is beyond a school's responsibility and inappropriate to specifically prescribe where a student or family should receive assessment or treatment, school wellbeing personnel are able to provide information to parents about the local services that are available.

What help is helpful?

Before we consider the different options for where schools can turn to get help for their students with emotional and behavioural health concerns, I'd like us to take a detour to ask the question, 'What help is actually helpful for students with emotional and behavioural concerns?' We need to start with realistic expectations about what 'help' can actually achieve. Unfortunately, in the field of mental health, we don't so much offer *cures* as we do *treatments*. Such treatments operate in one of four different ways. First, some treatments seek to *reduce the levels of symptoms*. Medications for ADHD, for example, help curb the impulsiveness of hyperactive young people. Second, some treatments help the sufferer *manage their symptoms more effectively* when they appear. Consider here the role of breathing techniques during panic attacks. Third, some treatments seek to *remove or reduce the precipitating factors* that can trigger a person's distress. One common example here is family therapy to change the parental or other family processes that can trigger or maintain a young person's difficulties. And finally, some treatments seek to *train and upskill* young people with new ways of coping with their life circumstances.

Of course, none of these things are the responsibility of school personnel. However, school staff who are seeking to link students with suitable help need to know what help is available and have some confidence that such help will make a difference for their students.

If I were writing this book in the early- and even mid-20th century, this section would be very brief. At that time, medical and psychological science had no *proven* way to help kids with emotional and behavioural disorders. Thankfully, since the late 1940s, we have seen some very significant advancement in treatments such that now we can have a degree of confidence that genuine, evidence-based help is available. These can be summarised within two broad categories: medicine and what we'll refer to here as 'talking therapies'. Let's consider them one at a time.

Medicine

Medicines for psychiatric illness are still very young in the history of the medical profession. At the time of the Second World War, we really had no effective psychiatric medications. All that changed in the 1949 when Australian John Cade published the first paper on the use of lithium for the treatment of bipolar disorder. Shortly after that, in France during the early 1950s, the first clinical trials of chlorpromazine as an antipsychotic were done. Since then, there has been a gradual but genuine proliferation of psychiatric medicines for use in both adults and children.

Getting help

As a rule, these medicines usually work by changing the biochemistry of the brain with different medicines acting on different brain neuroreceptors and chemicals. A broad range of medicines exists now for most common psychiatric disorders, including depression, anxiety, ADHD, psychosis and bipolar disorder. Aided by extensive research trials and well-documented clinical guidelines, the medical profession has become very skilful at tailoring the right medication to the right patient for the right condition.

Naturally, school personnel are not expected to know about the workings of different psychiatric medications. It can be helpful, however, to have some general knowledge about the types of medications students may be prescribed for different difficulties. They can be conveniently (although overly simplistically) grouped into five broad categories, as summarised in Table 9.1. This table comes with one crucial caveat: drugs from pretty much any of the medication groups listed are not infrequently used to treat conditions other than those listed in the table. For example, what I have listed as antidepressants are also frontline medicines for anxiety; many of the antipsychotic medicines are also effective with young people with bipolar disorder.[1]

Having said that, it is also important to recognise that medicines are not miracle remedies. They usually only provide partial relief of symptoms, their benefits can take some time to take effect, and all drugs have side effects. In fact, if a psychiatric medication can get even a 20–30% symptom

Table 9.1 Classes of Medications

Medication Group	Condition Treated	Generic Medicine Names (Brand Names)
Antidepressants	Depression	• Fluvoxamine (e.g. Luvox) • Sertraline (e.g. Zoloft) • Fluoxetine (e.g. Prozac)
Anxiolytics	Anxiety	• Alprazolam (e.g. Xanax) • Diazepam (e.g. Valium)
Stimulants	ADHD	• Amphetamines (e.g. Adderall) • Methylphenidate (e.g. Ritalin, Concerta) • Lisdexamfetamine (Vyvanse)
Antipsychotics	Psychosis/ schizophrenia	• Risperidone (e.g. Risperdal) • Quetiapine (e.g. Seroquel) • Aripiprazole (e.g. Abilify)
Mood stabilisers	Bipolar disorder	• Lithium Carbonate (e.g. Quilonum SR)

improvement, it is usually considered a 'win'. Imagine a student who failed a mathematics test. If, after an educational intervention, the student re-sat the exam and improved by 20–30%, we wouldn't necessarily be wildly celebrating, but we could say, 'Well, that's certainly better than what it was'. One final point to make is that medications are often not used alone but are used in conjunction with our other main form of intervention – talking therapies.

Talking therapies

'Talking therapies' is a collective term used to refer to therapies that involve talking. Someone stayed up late one night inventing that term! When Sigmund Freud developed psychoanalysis in the late 1800s, he truly revolutionised the field of mental health 'treatment', which, up until that time, had been characterised by high-technology therapies such as blood-letting, exorcisms, leeches, hydrotherapy[2] and confinement to asylums. Freud developed a comprehensive 'psychological' model to explain mental disorders, in contrast to many of the other extreme and unhelpful theories of his time. He developed the approach of a therapist sitting with a client and talking about their problems in a respectful and collaborative fashion.[3]

My profession owes are great deal to Dr Freud for this contribution, and, over the past hundred years, the field of 'psychotherapy' has flourished. Today's talking therapists come from a broad variety of professional backgrounds, including social work, counselling, psychology, nursing, medicine, chaplaincy and occupational therapy. Therapists from any of these professions can be excellent, and they all will come from a starting point of establishing a compassionate and empathic relationship with their client. Let's call this 'first base'. What decades of research has shown, however, is that this first base is usually not sufficient to achieve the 'home run' of significant improvement for young people with the types of complex emotional and behavioural disorders we are discussing in this book. Different approaches to talking therapies yield different results for different disorders. You may have heard of some of these therapies: cognitive behavioural therapy, acceptance and commitment therapy, dialectic behaviour therapy, family therapy, interpersonal psychotherapy, solution focused therapy and mindfulness-based cognitive therapy, to name just a few.

We need to make an important point here that will require a little explanation. Stick with me as we work towards a critical conclusion. To better understand this idea that not all approaches to talking therapies are equal, we need to dig a little into the concept of 'levels of evidence'. Various medical and research organisations have published classification systems for how much evidence exists to support a particular approach to intervention. In Australia, we usually use the levels of evidence defined by the National Health and Medical Research Council (NHMRC). These guidelines divide evidence into four hierarchical levels. The lowest form of evidence, Level 4, consists of published case studies that report on the outcome of an intervention with an individual or cohort. Slightly better is Level 3 evidence, which is derived from studies that compare intervention trials but without strong attention to control groups. Level 2 evidence is drawn from well-constructed randomised controlled with independent, blind comparison groups. At this point, we're starting to get some pretty good evidence. At the top of the evidence hierarchy, Level 1, is evidence that comes from the systematic review of the Level 2 studies. It is only once we get to Level 1 evidence that we can start to form some strong conviction of the efficacy – or otherwise – of any psychological intervention. You may have noticed that, in this book, as far as possible, I seek to site these systematic reviews and meta-analytic studies to support the points I am making.

The Australian Psychological Society periodically reviews the available evidence for psychological interventions for the treatment of mental disorders and summarises it according to the NHMRC levels of evidence.[4] Coming back to our baseball analogy, a sad reality is that talking therapies rarely *hit the ball out of the park* in terms of their effectiveness. And this is where the rubber hits the road for schools trying to work out which are the best counselling services to use for students with serious emotional and behavioural disorders. There is one form of talking therapy that stands out from the pack in terms of the Level 1 evidence: cognitive behavioural therapy. Hands down, it has the most convincing evidence for anxiety disorders, depression and behavioural disorders. This isn't to say that other talking therapies don't have some evidence or that they can't help. However, the take-home message for school personnel is, if you are looking to refer a student to a counselling practitioner, especially for anxiety, depression or behavioural disorders, the safest bet is to consider someone who practices cognitive behavioural therapy. You can usually have some reassurance that most hospital and university clinics will use evidenced-based practices. Moreover, it is quite common for individual therapists to advertise the type of talking therapy they offer.

Charlotte – Part 2

Collecting as much calm as she could, and fearing the response she would get, Bec asked Charlotte, 'Have you had thoughts of ending your own life?' Charlotte's gaze remained towards the floor, and she shrugged. Seeking clarification, Bec asked, 'Does that mean yes or no?' Again, she was greeted with a shrug. If there was any doubt before now, this moment confirmed for Bec that she was well out of her depth. This wasn't a job for a History teacher-come-Year Advisor. Bec told Charlotte that she understood that she was feeling miserable and that everything had become overwhelming for her. Bec also explained to Charlotte that she couldn't let her leave school until she knew that she was well enough and safe enough to go and that she'd need to call her mum to come to school to collect her. Another shrug. In the hour that it took to organise for Mrs Bonucci to get to school, Bec kept Charlotte closely supervised, made her a cup of tea, and they played a game of Uno. In her own mind, Bec was mulling over 'What now?' She knew it was right that Charlotte was transferred back into the care and supervision of her family. What she wanted to get straight, however, was what guidance to give Mrs Bonnuci about what to do now in order to get Charlotte properly looked after and make sure she was safe. The school had a good relationship with a local psychology clinic, but it would likely take weeks – or, more likely, months – to get an appointment. The school counsellor would be back at work on Monday, but that left Charlotte without help over the weekend. Anyway, Bec knew only too well the school counsellor's mantra that 'a school counselling service isn't a replacement for a mental health clinic'. She was left weighing the options of seeing a local general practitioner or even going directly to the emergency department of the local hospital when Mrs Bonucci knocked on the door. Bec thanked Mrs Bonucci for her willingness to come directly to school and gave her a factual overview of the events of the past hour. She tried to get Charlotte to engage in the conversation and explain how she was feeling, but Charlotte remained distant and non-communicative. Bec had anticipated Mrs Bonucci's first question: what do we need to do *now*? Bec gave an honest answer that she was not a mental health professional but that she firmly believed that Charlotte needed to be properly assessed by someone qualified to help them. Moreover, she stressed that they all needed to be sure that

Getting help

> Charlotte was not a risk to herself. At this point, Bec's mind became clear – this wasn't something to take risks with. 'Mrs Bonucci, I think you need to take Bec straight down to the local hospital. They have a mental health crisis team that will be able to help Charlotte today'. Bec expected that Charlotte would protest at this suggestion and try to reassure the adults that she was fine. The fact she didn't protest confirmed for Bec that Charlotte really did need professional help.

Getting help – where and how?

With some cautious optimism that medicinal and talking therapies can make a genuine difference in the lives of troubled young people, we will now move on to consider the range of options for community-based help that are available for schools, students and families. Upstream staff in schools should ensure that they have some familiarity with the options available within their community.

General practitioners

As we explore the range of options available in the landscape of community-based services, our first stop is with general practitioners (or family/primary care physicians). I'm hoping you won't mind me taking a brief and nostalgic detour as I reflect on the work of my own father as an 'old school' general practitioner (GP). My dad worked in the same medical practice in suburban Sydney for four decades. He was the type of GP that delivered the babies of the babies he had delivered 25 years earlier. He was the type of GP who would get called out in the middle of the night to see patients who didn't know who else to call. He was the type of GP who was showered with gifts each Christmas, as his patients sought to express their gratitude for all his help over the course of the year.

I have fond memories as a kid of being in the passenger seat of his car as he would make house calls on the way home from wherever we had been. I remain very proud of my dad and the care, commitment and professionalism that characterised his approach to his patients. I remember him explaining to me as a kid that 'GPs know a little bit of stuff about lot of things, while specialists know a lot of stuff about one thing'. His explanation, of course, is simplistic, but it's important for making the point that we need to address here: GPs know about a lot of stuff . . . including mental health.

It is also true to say that the medical landscape has changed dramatically since my dad was practicing such that mental health is now one of the things that GPs know best. Since 2017, the Royal Australian College of General Practice has released an annual report called *The General Practice Health of the Nation*, which contains the results of a national survey of their members.[5] One thing they report on each year is the primary presenting problems that are being seen by GPs. When my dad was in practice, the types of complaints that would have topped the list would be things like hypertension, dermatology, sprains and breaks, and obstetric and gynaecological concerns. Not so anymore! The number one reason for patient presentation to GPs in every survey since 2017 is (do I even need to say it?) psychological! This was the case regardless of geographical location, gender, socioeconomic status and even the age of the GP. Moreover, each year, the percentage of patients presenting with psychological concerns is growing, from 61% in 2017 to 71% by 2022.

The point to be made, then, is that GPs are very experienced in helping people with mental health concerns. Young people and their families can expect GPs to conduct an assessment of the young person's mental state, provide initial support and advice, and determine what type of intervention is indicated going forward. One thing we can expect of a good GP is that they will be well acquainted with the other community-based mental health services in the area. They will have a good working relationship with the local paediatricians, psychiatrists, psychologists and counsellors and, when necessary, facilitate a referral.

Community-based mental health clinics

The bulk of the 'heavy lifting' for child and adolescent mental health counselling comes through community-based mental health clinics. Although each school will have slightly different systems for how they progress students along the pathway to care towards community-based services, it is important that any wellbeing staff who are part of this process know something of the range of services available through the local mental health clinics. Such clinics come in a wide variety of formats and tend to be embarrassingly plentiful in affluent parts of the world and distressingly scarce in the less affluent areas. Common points of differentiation include whether they

Getting help

are privately or publicly operated, whether they charge for their services, whether a referral is required, and the wait time to get an appointment. The other point of differentiation concerns those who staff the service and what training and qualifications they hold. Here, things can get murky as members of the public frequently don't understand the difference between different types of mental health professionals. The point I made earlier, however, is that just as important as the professional background of practitioner is the approach they bring to their work.

Telephone helplines

We should never underestimate the vital role that telephone helplines play in the mental health safety net for young people. During the school day, students are surrounded by caring staff who they can talk to, should they choose to do so. The reality, however, is that many young people get most distressed out of school hours and frequently late at night. Accordingly, reminding our at-risk students about the service offered by these free helplines, including how to access them, is one practical and important step that schools can take.

We also need to understand the limitations of these helplines – that is, what they *don't* offer. Telephone helplines are not staffed by qualified mental health professionals. Rather, they are usually volunteers with basic training in how to listen and empathise, to offer some basic guidance on coping with strong emotion and to direct the young person to emergency care if they believe the young person is at risk of harm. The important point to make here is that telephone crisis lines are in no way a substitute for comprehensive, ongoing therapy from a fully trained mental health professional. Telephone help lines are a fabulous adjunct to ongoing therapy, but they are not sufficient for genuinely unwell students.

Hospital emergency departments

Most of us know that we can visit hospital emergency departments (EDs) in the event of an urgent *physical* health problem, such as a serious traumatic wound, a heart attack or a severe asthma attack. What many of us don't know is that most major hospitals are also set up to manage *mental* health emergencies. It is important that we remember that EDs are for genuine emergencies. Just as we wouldn't go to an ED with a sore throat, likewise, we shouldn't go to the ED for emotional and behavioural concerns unless the situation represents a genuine emergency.

There are three main scenarios that school staff might encounter that fall within the category of a genuine 'emergency'. The first is with a student who is expressing an active and imminent intention to end their own life. There is a distinction to be made here with students who experience suicidal ideation but have no particular intention to act on their thoughts. Students like this require close supervision and professional assessment but may not need to be taken directly to the ED.

By contrast, consider Jake, a 14-year-old boy from a country town who was living in the boarding house of a school where I was working. One Monday morning, during a routine counselling session, Jake revealed to me that he was having suicidal thoughts. Worse than that, before school that morning, he had taken some steps to end his own life. His plans were only thwarted by his own chilling calculation that the method he had planned would not actually be lethal. As we spoke, Jake could offer me no reasons to want to live and no guarantees that he would not take further steps to end his life. This constituted a genuine emergency. I made two phone calls instantly. The first was to the principal of our school to let them know about my extreme concern for Jake. The second was to call a taxi. A colleague and I immediately transported Jake to the local ED, where we stayed until Jake's parents were able to meet us and take over responsibility. Jake was admitted to the hospital for further assessment, supervision and care.

The second and related scenario when a school might directly take a student to the ED is following incidents of significant self-harm. As we learned in Chapter 8, when a student is known to have self-harmed at school, it is very reasonable for school staff to ask about the nature of the self-harm and to examine any injury in order to apply first aid. Depending on the circumstances, any student reporting ingesting substances will likely be required to go to the ED or have an ambulance called. Similarly, any self-harm resulting in significant blood loss may also require immediate emergency intervention.

The third scenario when school staff might take a student to the ED is when that student is having a psychotic episode, evidenced by bizarre behaviour, delusions or hallucinations, or obvious disorganised thinking. Such students represent a very real danger to themselves and possibly to other students, particularly if, in a deluded state, they believe they possess skills that could be highly dangerous (for example, believing they can fly) or they are hearing voices directing them to hurt themselves or others. These students need school staff to remain calm, maintain constant supervision and transition them to immediate care. In fact, there will be times when these students require more immediate attention that falls more appropriately into our next category of help.

Dial emergency

All the sources of help described so far have one thing in common: they assume that the student is not an immediate threat to themselves or others. In most situations, schools and parents together can take steps, sometimes pressing and rapid steps, to link a young person with suitable community services. Sometimes, however, the situation is so urgent that the school will need to call the local emergency number for the assistance of police and/or ambulance. A few years ago, at a school where I was working, a 15-year-old boy known to have a range of mental health concerns was spotted by some fellow students on a window ledge at the top of one of the school's tallest buildings. Let's not even begin to entertain the scenarios of Hollywood movies, where the protagonist climbs up to the rooftop and, with heartfelt words, is able to talk the suicidal character down from the roof. There is no mental health first aid for these scenarios other than an immediate call to the police and emergency services. School staff need to be prepared to concisely relay the nature of the scenario that requires an emergency response. As per usual first aid protocols, school staff should also consider what danger the scenario presents to other members of the school community and take action to ensure their safety. On a large school site, staff should be deployed to the school gate to then direct the emergency services to the location of the emergency.

What to do when students and parents refuse help

Our discussion to date is predicated on the assumption that our students and families are willing to seek help. There is another group of students and families that we need to consider: those who *refuse* to seek help even when the school is firmly of the view that help is required. We saw in an earlier chapter that there are various reasons why people refuse help. But at the end of the day, a school can't force a student to seek external help. I want to offer five responses the school can make in these situations.

1. Seek to understand resistance

People don't refuse to seek help just to be difficult. In their mind, there is a reasonable (to their way of thinking) explanation for their reluctance. One helpful response from the school is to seek to understand this reluctance. Some students or parents will be only too quick to tell you their reasoning. At other times, students or parents have more personal reasons that they may not have made obvious. It is perfectly reasonable for a school to ask, 'Can you help us understand why you don't want to get help?'

The trick here is to ensure that, in your dealings to date, you have not given the student or family reason to think that you are judging them for their actions. In the context of a non-judgmental relationship, the student or parent may be willing to open up about their reasons. On many occasions in schools I've worked in, once we've better understood a family's reluctance to seek help, we have been able to find ways to address their concerns and organise external help.

2. Plan a follow-up meeting

It is inevitable that things will change over time. When a student or parent declines the school's strong recommendation to get external help, I suggest inviting them to have a follow-up meeting to review progress. This means that your recommendation hasn't hit a dead end. There is still a chance to review progress and make further recommendations down the track. Perhaps, over the ensuing time, the student will improve, making the external referral unnecessary. Perhaps they will deteriorate, and the family will see that the referral has merit. A follow-up meeting means you are still in the game.

3. Ensure reasonable school-based care

When a school holds a concern for a student who won't seek external help, the school can implement additional reasonable levels of care and supervision. A careful balancing act is required here. On one hand, the school may be able to mobilise the *reasonable temporary* resources of a school counsellor or check-ins with a homeroom teacher or Year Advisor. On the other hand, schools should not feel responsible for the ongoing overall mental health and wellbeing of the student.

4. 'One small step'

Sometimes, children and families don't need to see an external specialist to start to make some positive changes in their lives. As a psychologist, I will nearly always set my clients 'homework' to do between meetings. Actually, I'll often ask *them* to set *themselves* some homework. I ask them to think of 'one small step' that they could do in the coming week that might help them cope better with the predicament that they face. That's a question anyone can ask. No matter how large the challenge that a student or family face, the path forward will always start with one small step. It is not a guarantee of substantial change, but you might be surprised how frequently one small step can set a chain reaction in place. To the degree that the student or family choose their own homework, they are also more likely to carry out their choice.

5. Report to child welfare

In all jurisdictions I am aware of, refusal to seek help in the face of significant risk to child wellbeing triggers a mandatory obligation for school staff to report the child to the state welfare authorities. At this point, we come back to the importance of a careful risk assessment that balances the impact and the likelihood of harm. A student and/or parent refusing to seek help in the face of significant risk can leave the school with no choice but to make a report to the relevant child welfare authority.

Concluding thoughts

And so, we've reached the climax of this book. Everything we've learnt so far has been to get us to this point – the point where we link students who need help with suitable services in the community in a timely fashion. Our focus in this chapter has been on becoming familiar with what help is available and facilitating the journey towards that help. There are some concluding thoughts to make before we move on to our final chapter.

Cultural considerations in mental health

We all have differing views on mental health and mental illness. To a large degree, these are shaped by our racial and cultural backgrounds. Stemming from this, as we discuss emotional and behavioural concerns with students and their families, we must do two things. The first is to be aware of *our own preconceptions* around mental health and understand that not everyone thinks the same way that we do – and that's fine. And the second thing is to be aware of the *student and family's preconceptions.* Although we will be careful to not make uninformed assumptions, we should expect that families from European, Asian, African or American backgrounds will all bring differing expectations around mental illness. First Nations people will hold views on health and family and spirituality that will influence their actions around help-seeking. We must be sensitive to the deep shame and stigma that many cultures still associate with mental illness. We might also find that students born to migrant families may hold different views to those held by their parents, and this too may be a hurdle to be navigated.

The practical implication here is to seek to connect, as far as possible, students and families with services that are culturally relevant and sensitive. Families may have a preference to meet with a community-based service provider who speaks their language or who shares their faith. There may be specialty services available for particular minorities, including ethnic and migrant groups or services for LGBTQI+ youth. When we encounter resistance about engaging with external mental health services, these cultural considerations could be one barrier to navigate.

Telehealth

There isn't much good that we can say about the COVID-19 pandemic. One way in which the world did advance, however, was in our fast-tracking of teleconferencing technology in the delivery of health care services. Telehealth was available before COVID but took off as the world sought ways to allow people access to health practitioners during lockdown. In many ways, telehealth is more suited to the delivery of mental health services than physical health services in that mental health clinicians don't have the same need to physically assess body ailments. And now, as we tentatively move forward in the post-COVID world, we continue to make strong use of telehealth in the delivery of mental health services.

Getting help

This has opened up an entirely new range of possibility for how those in need can access counselling. People can access specialist mental health services without leaving home. People living in rural and remote areas can access mental health services based in the cities. Without the need to hire physical premises, some clinicians can pass cost benefits on to their clients. Ongoing use of telehealth creates an additional pathway for students needing to access care.

Online interventions

I am firmly of the view that the best help for distressed young people is meeting with an experienced mental health professional for further assessment and to develop an intervention plan. We have acknowledged, however, that frequently that option is not available due to the paucity of services in the local area, long wait lists, prohibitive costs, or resistance from students and families to attend those services. An alternate approach to help that has gained momentum is web-based mental health interventions. In essence, these are psycho-educational programs that teach young people and/or their parents about the causes of emotional and behavioural problems and instruct them in the skills that help alleviate their symptoms. They have been shown to be most effective for internalising rather than externalising disorders.

The best-known digital program for depression is *Moodgym*, developed at the Australian National University. *Moodgym* is an interactive program that teaches teenagers and young adults self-help skills for managing symptoms of depression and anxiety. The best-known program for anxiety in children is *CoolKids Online*, developed at Macquarie University. The *CoolKids* program is designed to teach parents and children together how to manage anxiety and face their fears. *CoolKids* has a sibling program for teenagers called *Chilled Out*. Another well-known anxiety program is the *Brave Program*, developed at the University of Queensland. I mention the university of origin for these programs to indicate that they have been extensively researched and found to be effective. Importantly, they are all based on the cognitive behavioural therapy approach that we have already discussed in this chapter. Online programs such as these are not suitable as crisis intervention, or for students with severe symptoms but can be a valuable alternative source of help for those with less severe symptoms and those who can't access face-to-face clinicians.

In a nutshell

- It is not a school's core responsibility to provide assessment and treatment for students with emotional and behavioural disorders.
- Schools are excellently placed to facilitate getting students who need help to suitable community-based mental health providers. This is normally done by alerting parents of the school's concerns and encouraging help-seeking.
- Mental health interventions don't 'cure' emotional and behavioural disorders, but they can make a substantial improvement in the life of the young person and lower their risk of harm. Medicine and talking therapies are the two main approaches on offer.
- There is a range of different community-based options available for schools to refer to, including GPs, telephone support lines, mental health clinics, hospitals and emergency services.
- Even if students and parents refuse to seek help, there are ways the school can help.
- Whenever possible, we are best to link students and families with services that are appropriate to their ethnic and cultural background.
- Web-based interventions are a good alternative for students with less severe symptoms who may not access clinicians directly.

Digging Deeper

1 If you really want to geek out on classification systems for psychotropic medications, in 1976 the World Health Organisation developed a system called the Anatomical Therapeutic Chemical system, which divided drugs into groups depending on the body organ or system on which they act. More recently, a group of neuropsychopharmacology organisations developed an alternate system called the Neuroscience-based Nomenclature (NbN) that classifies drugs according to their pharmacology and mechanisms of action. Satisfy your inner geek at the NbN website: https://nbn2r.com/

2 We are not referring here to contemporary therapy used, for example, by physiotherapists during rehabilitation after physical trauma but instead the use of baths, showers and sprays of different temperatures to heal mental illness.

Getting help

3 Unfortunately, some the actual content of Dr Freud's theories is now considered at best unscientific and at worst downright 'wacky'. But that's a story for another day.

4 If you can't sleep one night, or, if you are like me and find this stuff interesting, you can dig into this here: The Australian Psychological Society. (2018). *Evidence-based psychological interventions in the treatment of mental disorders.* https://psychology.org.au/getmedia/23c6a11b-2600-4e19-9a1d-6ff9c2f26fae/evidence-based-psych-interventions.pdf

5 Read it for yourself here: https://www.racgp.org.au/health-of-the-nation/health-of-the-nation

10 Self-care for school staff

Barney

From his very first year as a graduate teacher, Barney Hardin knew that the final few weeks of the academic year were the most gruelling. He often wondered why school administrators couldn't find some way to spread the workload more evenly across the year. At the end of the semester, when he was most exhausted, he had to plough his way through marking 120 calculus exams and then write all his end-of-term report comments. Now a middle-aged man, Barney was well aware that he had neither the energy nor the enthusiasm that he had as a younger teacher. He secretly resented those organised and conscientious teachers in his faculty who had done first drafts of the report comments many weeks ago. He was also aware that his life was more complicated now than it had been just a few years ago. His father had been left incapacitated following a stroke and now required regular additional care. Barney was going to his parents' house two or three afternoons each week to assist with showering, shopping and generally checking on his mother. The demands of the job, coupled with his time spent at his parents' house, had taken a toll on his own family. He knew his wife and kids were not getting the attention that they deserved. Not infrequently, his wife would remind him of this. He knew he wasn't his usual self, but he didn't know what else to do. In these final weeks of Term, he would leave school with the very best of intentions to power through marking the Year 10 exams so he could then start his reports. However, by the time he got home, after a 90-minute detour to his parents, the best he could muster was to get a beer from the fridge, collapse onto the lounge,

> and turn his mind to 'off' while watching some depressing current affairs on the TV. Some nights, one beer became two or three or more. 'I'll set the alarm and get up early in the morning' was his Plan B. After a poor night's sleep, Plan B rarely eventuated, and he arrived at school the next day rushed, unprepared and more stressed than he had left the day before. If Barney had been in a clearer headspace, he would have realised that this cycle wasn't sustainable. He felt trapped but saw no way out. He didn't realise quite how out of control he was until the incident that threatened to end his teaching career. It was a Thursday afternoon, last class for the day. This Year 9 class had been chatty all year, and Tyson Johnson had a defiant streak that tested the patience of even the most unflappable teacher. A few impertinent remarks from the back of the room had already prompted Barney to move Tyson to a desk at the front of the class, directly next to the whiteboard. Barney turned to his whiteboard with a large plastic compass he was using to create circles for his geometry lesson. One loud fart from Tyson was all it took. Barney snapped! He swung the compass forcefully down onto Tyson's desk. He hadn't considered that Tyson's fingers would be on the desk at the exact spot where the compass landed. In his stressed fury he didn't stop to consider anything. Tyson's knuckles absorbed the full force of the compass. He screamed in pain. The entire class gasped in shock. Barney was instantly flooded with horror at his own actions. Jumping to his feet, Tyson shrieked, 'You've broken by hand!'

The teaching profession has an internationally recognised, critical problem – namely, teacher attrition and retention rates. This isn't a new problem, but it is certainly one that has gained concerning momentum in recent years. Put simply, the number of teachers exiting the back door are more numerous than those coming in the front door. Education systems around the world are desperately trying to work out how to address this problem.

One of the best ways of understanding what is happening to the teaching profession on an international level is through the data provided by the TALIS research, that we met in Chapter 1. A core question asked in the TALIS survey related to whether teachers were satisfied with their profession. A worrying trend across many countries, including England, New Zealand, Denmark and Israel, was a decrease in teacher satisfaction with their profession. For the record, in the five-year reporting period, there was no significant deterioration in satisfaction in my home country of Australia.

TALIS also asked teachers about the extent to which they experienced stress in their work. On average, 18% of teachers reported the top response of 'a lot' of stress, but this rate leapt to above 30% for teachers in England, Portugal and Hungary and 28% for teachers in Australia. TALIS also reported the sources of teacher stress within three broad categories, which I suspect will resonate loudly with those reading this book. The first category related to workload with top concerns being the amount of administrative work to do as well as having too much marking. The second source was related to student behaviour, such as being held responsible for students' achievement and maintaining classroom discipline. The third area was termed 'responsiveness to stakeholders' with the primary stressors including keeping up with changing requirements from local and national educational authorities as well as addressing parent or guardian expectations.

While TALIS doesn't report data from the United States, the title of a recent Rand Corporation research report in the United States tells the tale bluntly enough: Stress Topped the Reasons Why Public School Teachers Quit, Even Before COVID-19.[1] The study found that the 'teacher leavers' in their sample left for both COVID-19-specific reasons and for other longstanding structural problems in the profession. They specifically cited the long work hours, lack of flexibility in work schedules, poor work climate and the somewhat low rates of pay relative to the demands of the job. Unless steps are taken to adequately counteract these stresses, the profession will continue to lose outstanding educators.

Our job in this book isn't to solve the international teacher-shortage crisis or to find answers to all the stresses of the profession. Rather, the point to be made is the simple reality that is no doubt already painfully evident to you – teaching is a stressful profession. It's a profession where, if you don't take intentional steps to look after yourself, you are likely to join the exodus out the back door. In this chapter, we will consider the importance of self-care for educators and review the core components of an evidence-based self-care plan.

Burnout: Am I at risk?

At this point, I want to take a brief detour to consider the question, 'How would I know if I was at risk of burning out or indeed already there?' There have been countless definitions of burnout, but for our purposes here I like the simple and no-nonsense description provided some years ago by burnout scholars Wilmar Schaufeli and Esther Greenglass: 'a state of physical, emotional and mental exhaustion that results from long-term involvement in work situations that are emotionally demanding'.[2] A sad reality for many people is that we are not good at knowing or noticing our own signs of burnout. Like the proverbial frog in boiling water, our stress levels slowly rise over weeks, months and years, and we don't realise that we are at a boiling point until it is too late.

To remedy this, I want to offer the chance to complete a quick burnout inventory. Completing this inventory is helpful for two reasons. The first is that it is educational: it provides a list of the common symptoms of burnout. The second is that it is self-evaluating: it provides a chance to reflect on your own experience of these 'symptoms' and ask, 'Could I be at risk of burnout?'

The Copenhagen Burnout Inventory (CBI) is a widely used and well validated research and clinical questionnaire to measure individual burnout.[3] It consists of three separate sub-domains that measure different components of burnout: personal burnout (Table 10.1), work-related burnout (Table 10.2)

Table 10.1 Personal Burnout: The degree of physical and psychological fatigue and exhaustion that you experience

	Always	Often	Sometimes	Seldom	Never/ almost never
How often do you feel tired?					
How often are you physically exhausted?					
How often are you emotionally exhausted?					
How often do you think: 'I can't take it any more'?					
How often do you feel worn out?					
How often do you feel weak and susceptible to illness?					
Total score = add together your scores for all six questions					
Final Score: Divide the total score by six [Total score/6]					

Self-care for school staff

Table 10.2 Work-Related Burnout: The degree of physical and psychological fatigue and exhaustion that you perceive related to your work

	Always	Often	Sometimes	Seldom	Never/almost never
Do you feel worn out at the end of the working day?					
Are you exhausted in the morning at the thought of another day at work?					
Do you feel that every working hour is tiring for you?					
Do you have enough energy for family and friends during leisure time?*					
	To a very high degree	To a high degree	Somewhat	To a low degree	To a very low degree
Is your work emotionally exhausting?					
Does your work frustrate you?					
Do you feel burnt out because of your work?					
Total score = add together your scores for all seven questions					
Final Score: Divide the total score by seven [Total score/7]					

* NOTE: When you are scoring this question, you need to reverse your answers. That is, if you answered 'Always', then score this as 0; if you responded 'Never/Almost Never', score this as 100; and similarly, swap around the scores for the 'Often' and 'Seldom' responses.

and client-related burnout (Table 10.3). Definitions of each of these domains are provided in their corresponding tables. You can complete the CBI questions in these tables by placing a tick in response option (Always, Often, Sometimes, Seldom, Never/Almost Never) that best represents your experience of the questions asked. Where you see the word 'client', consider this

Self-care for school staff

Table 10.3 Client-Related Burnout: The degree of physical and psychological fatigue and exhaustion that you perceive related to your work with clients

	Always	Often	Some-times	Seldom	Never/almost never
Are you tired of working with clients?					
Do you sometimes wonder how long you will be able to continue working with clients?					

	To a very high degree	To a high degree	Somewhat	To a low degree	To a very low degree
Do you find it hard to work with clients?					
Does it drain your energy to work with clients?					
Do you find it frustrating to work with clients?					
Do you feel that you give more than you get back when you work with clients?					
Total score = add together your scores for all six questions					
Final Score: Divide the total score by six [Total score/6]					

to mean the students (and/or parents or staff if they are a significant part of your 'client' base) that you work with.

Scoring and interpreting the CBI

Now, let's score your CBI and make sense of what is to be learned from your answers. First, give each of your answers a score according to the following score key:

Always/ To a very high degree	100
Often/ To a high degree	75
Sometimes/ Somewhat	50
Seldom/ To a low degree	25
Never/Almost Never/ To a very low degree	0

Next, add up all your scores for each subdomain and write the Total Score in the space at the bottom of each subdomain table. Finally, divide each of the Total Scores by the number of questions in each subdomain (six in the personal and client-related subdomains and seven in the work-related subdomain) to provide an *average* score for each subdomain. Scores can range from 0 to 100, but, for most of us, the scores will average somewhere between 25 and 75. Of course our responses will change from day to day depending on what is going on in our lives. Moreover, the developers of the CBI make very clear that there is no special 'cutoff' score that delineates between those who are burned out and those who are not. Rather, scores should be considered as broad-brush guidelines along a continuum. With this in mind, we can say that average scores below 50 on each subdomain are not suggestive of burnout; average scores of 50 to 74 may suggest moderate burnout; and average scores above 75 may suggest high levels of burnout. Where does this place your burnout levels, and which subdomains are more concerning for you?

Keep your burnout scores in mind as we now shift our attention to considering how we can better care for ourselves. The self-care strategies that we examine next will be useful as *remediation measures* to help bring our lives back into balance if we already feel some degree of stress and burnout but are best considered as *preventative measures* to help ensure we don't burnout.

What is self-care?

I define self-care as the intentional, pre-emptive habits that we establish to maximise our wellbeing. In this definition, we see five vital components:

1. *Intentional*: The practices of good self-care simply won't happen if we take a 'wait and hope' approach. Good self-care is too important to be left to chance. Instead, it is founded in intentional choices that are carefully planned to bring a desired effect.
2. *Pre-emptive*: The best self-care activities are pre-emptive in that they occur before a problem has taken hold. Prevention is always better than the cure. That said, the strategies we consider here are equally relevant if you are already feeling some degree of stress or burnout.
3. *Habits*: Without doubt humans are creatures of habit. Once an action becomes a habit, it is much more likely to continue to happen. Self-care is about establishing routines in our lives – daily, weekly, monthly – that gradually, over time, become the natural rhythms of our lives which enhance wellbeing.
4. *Maximise*: We all have better days and worse days, better weeks and worse weeks. That is normal. Self-care isn't aimed at *eliminating* stress or problems. Rather, it is aimed at maximising our wellbeing in the face of these stresses and problems.
5. *Wellbeing*: Defining wellbeing is a field within itself and a distraction from our core purposes here. The current buzzwords of 'flourishing' and 'thriving' are attractive ways of understanding wellbeing. You won't be surprised to hear that, as a psychologist, I am particularly interested in the emotional side of wellbeing. However, any good definition of wellbeing will take a broad view that includes the physical, emotional, social, spiritual, vocational and economic elements. These elements are all inter-related to the degree that a disturbance within one element will have direct consequences in other domains. Good self-care – indeed, good wellbeing – is necessarily wholistic.

The reasons for self-care

Why practice self-care? I want to offer three reasons that I hope will convince you to take self-care seriously. The first answer is obvious: we all want to have a life that minimises distress and maximises contentment. I want that for me, and I'm sure you want that for you. None of us want a life characterised by stress, sleeplessness, irritability, depression and so on. We all want that sense of balance in life such that we find our work stimulating and rewarding but then have the energy and 'headspace' to throw ourselves into our other passions and interests when we are not working. Whoever we are and whatever we do, adequate attention to self-care makes our lives better.

The second reason to prioritise self-care falls more directly in line with the core business of schools and educators. There is a preliminary but growing evidence base that teacher burnout is associated with lower student academic achievement and motivation. This is best highlighted in a systematic review published by Daniel Madigan and Lisa Kim, two scholars from York in the United Kingdom.[4] Their review of the literature uncovered 14 published studies that directly addressed this topic. Their disturbing conclusion was that 'students being taught by a teacher suffering from burnout tend to perform worse on exams, tests, and receive lower cumulative grades, than those taught by teachers not experiencing burnout' (p. 9). Reasons for this are not totally clear but most likely relate to burnt out teachers putting less effort into lesson planning, being less effective at classroom control and having worse relationships with their students. Regardless of reasons, teachers who want to maximise their student's performance should prioritise their own emotional wellbeing.

As much as I hope educators can enjoy 'the good life' (argument 1) and produce high-achieving students (argument 2), there is a third reason it is critical that school staff practice good self-care – a reason that is more connected to the purposes of this book. Only quite recently have researchers begun to investigate the relationship between teacher wellbeing and student wellbeing. Are they related, and if so, how? In 2016, Eva Oberle and Kimberley Schonert-Reichl from the University of British Columbia published a simple study with a powerful conclusion.[5] They measured teachers' burnout levels through an inventory very similar to the one we just did and then measured their students' stress levels via salivary cortisol levels. Concerningly, they found that higher levels of teacher burnout significantly predicted variability in their students' cortisol levels. Studies in the United Kingdom and Germany have also begun to establish this critical connection between the wellbeing of teachers and that of their students.[6] These findings support the 'stress contagion theory', that stress can be *caught* from those around us. The concern in a classroom context is that the stress of the tired, under-resourced and overwhelmed teacher leads to a deterioration in classroom climate, resulting in more problematic student behaviour, which, in turn, contributes to greater teacher stress. This is a cycle we want to avoid at all costs.

What does evidence-based self-care look like?

The rest of this chapter is devoted to describing what good self-care looks like. As you read this chapter, my hope is that you might be making two mental checklists. The first is called 'good self-care practices that I'm already doing'. Your job here is to ensure you *keep doing* these. The second list is called 'self-care practices that I'm not doing yet'. Your job here is to consider which self-care practices are likely to help you and *start doing* these things.

Self-care is not a 'one size fits all' approach. Instead, it is a matter of developing the practices that are relevant to the stresses in our lives and to our individual personalities and interests. What I will present here, however, are self-care strategies that have an evidence base to recommend them. It could be considered like the recipe for a meal, containing a description of a bunch of ingredients which, when combined, will become a satisfying and nutritious meal. You are, of course, very welcome to leave out some ingredients, add a few of your own favourites and cook it up in the way that works best for you. The key point, though, it that the recipe is not the meal. *Reading* these ideas won't magically reduce your stress or bring balance into your life. The challenge for you is to take this 'recipe', formulate a plan that has merit for you and then set about establishing your new self-care habits. That takes work and focus. We will come back to that point at the end of the chapter.

There are four main ingredients in this self-care recipe we will look at:

- Lifestyle factors
- Mindfulness-based stressed reduction
- Addressing work stressors
- Getting help

Lifestyle factors

If you were to read only one section of this entire book, this is the section I would have you read. My number one recommendation for how to best look after the mental health of your students is to look after your own mental health through establishing healthy lifestyle habits in your daily and weekly routine. The benefits of regular physical exercise, a healthy diet and a good night's sleep might sound like quaint wisdom from a bygone era, but these things are also 'hard core' evidence-based practices in the fight against stress and burnout. In our exploration of good self-care techniques, we will explore these three behemoths one at a time.

Physical exercise

Whenever I am designing a stress management program with senior high school students, the first 'ingredient' we look to include is invariably physical exercise. Exercise has the potential to influence our emotional health through both physiological and psychological mechanisms. *Physiological mechanisms* include benefits from the release of endorphins, increased production of mitochondria, increased levels of the neurotransmitters involved in wellbeing (serotonin, dopamine and noradrenaline) and modulating the activity of the hypothalamic-pituitary-adrenal system. *Psychological mechanisms* include the potential for exercise to distract and detach us from the worries of our workday as well as benefits to our mood, self-esteem and self-efficacy from completing and mastering an effortful task.[7] Physical exercise also promotes sounder sleep and enhanced cognitive function. I don't know of an easier or more powerful intervention to reduce stress. Most importantly, a stack of research has now highlighted the power of physical exercise specifically in benefiting educators.[8]

The problem many of us face, however, especially the further along the tunnel of burnout we get, is finding the time and energy to actually do any physical exercise. Getting up earlier in the day to exercise isn't appealing to anyone; the workday is too frenetic to contemplate squeezing in an additional activity; and, at the end of the day, we are too exhausted to do anything more than cook an evening meal and collapse. Oh, and that doesn't include getting our marking done and preparing for tomorrow's classes, taking out the garbage bins, taking the kids to soccer practice, then fighting with them about homework or piano practice (or whatever it is in your household), hearing about the joys and dramas in our partner's day, doing the dishes, fixing the dodgy Wi-Fi, or whatever it is that needs doing at your place after work. The reality is that you won't find that extra 30 minutes each day sitting around and waiting to be used. Instead, it will require a good degree of determination to make the exercise happen. And while, in my line of work, nothing comes with guarantees, I can all but guarantee that you will see rewards for any efforts you put into making time to exercise. Moreover, to the degree that you can sustain your efforts over time, you'll find that the determination required becomes much less as the days go by.

Some purists might push you towards specific types of exercise that have a more convincing evidence base. My recommendation, though, is that you chose to do an exercise that fulfils two key criteria. First, it must be *enjoyable*. Do something you like doing – plain and simple. Second, it must be *sustainable*. Sustainability will tap into what you have access to do (if you need to drive an hour to get to a pool, swimming probably isn't for you) and what your body can manage doing on a regular basis (don't plan on running 50 miles a day, every day). Beyond that, anything that gives your muscles and your cardiovascular system a workout is great – get to it! Later in this chapter, we'll have more to say about moving from theory to practice with your self-care plan.

Diet

Stress can lead us to overeat or to undereat. Moreover, the more stressed we become, the less likely we are to put the required effort into preparing healthy, balanced meals. Whether we eat too much, too little or just plain too 'junky', we are not providing our bodies with the necessary nutrients for wellbeing. Moreover, poor diet places additional strains on all our body systems and subsequently increases the risk for various chronic illnesses.

While the relationship between diet and physical health is well established, the effect of diet on mental health is comparatively new. In fact, the growing weight of interest and evidence in this area has led to the development of the new field of *nutritional psychiatry*.[9] Eating for mental health isn't about jumping on board a new diet doing the rounds on the internet and endorsed by Hollywood A-listers. By and large, it is a 'back to basics' approach to eating with the most convincing evidence found in the *Mediterranean diet*.[10]

You are probably familiar with the ubiquitous healthy-eating pyramid. What you may not know is that said pyramid was developed by the Harvard School of Public Health and the World Health Organisation in 1993 to summarise the traditional diets of people living around the Mediterranean Sea who were found to have lower rates of chronic illness and higher life expectancy than many other countries, even in the face of limited access to good health care. The Mediterranean diet is not complex and involves focusing on eating fruits and vegetables, cereals (whole grain cereals that is, not Coco-Pops or Rice Bubbles), nuts and healthy fats (olive oil being recommended) while adding moderate intake of fish as a primary protein source, poultry, eggs and dairy.[11]

As we consider diet, burnout and wellbeing, we also need to consider the elephant in the room – the use of alcohol and other drugs. For many people, alcohol can become a strategy for unwinding at the end of a stressful day. Teachers are not immune to this. The reasons why this 'solution' is in fact a 'problem' are well known:

- The addictive quality of alcohol means that, over time, more is required to achieve the same effect.
- Alcohol, even in small quantities, can be hazardous to various body organs.
- Despite some initial calming effects, alcohol acts as a depressant on the central nervous system and so ultimately makes us feel worse.
- Alcohol impairs sleep quality and hence undermines the restorative qualities of sleep.
- Going to work with a hangover will only inhibit our work performance the next day, making us less equipped to manage our stressors.
- Alcohol consumption can place strain on our relationships with friends and family, thus creating additional stress.
- Alcohol consumption does nothing to change the sources of our stress.

If any or all of these factors resonate for you, this is a good indication that your self-care plan will need to make some changes with how you use alcohol.

Sleep

Perhaps the most attractive aspect of incorporating sleep into our burnout-busting lifestyle is that, unlike exercise and diet, sleep requires no effort, no expense and no special equipment. Many of us will concur with the beauty and the ease of a good night's sleep. All it takes is the simple act of putting your head on a pillow and waiting, right? Sadly, however, for many of us it is not so simple, and a good night's sleep is elusive and rare.

The two international 'heavy hitters' in the field of sleep research, the American Academy of Sleep Medicine and the Sleep Research Society, have issued a joint consensus statement on how much sleep the average adult needs. Their statement, in part, reads:

> Adults should sleep 7 or more hours per night on a regular basis to promote optimal health. Sleeping less than 7 hours per night on a regular basis is associated with adverse health outcomes, including weight gain and obesity, diabetes, hypertension, heart disease and stroke, depression, and increased risk of death. Sleeping less than 7 hours per night is also associated with impaired immune function, increased pain, impaired performance, increased errors, and greater risk of accidents.[12]

This is a sobering cocktail of risks and should be enough to alert us to take sleep seriously. Usually, sleep difficulties can be ameliorated by good 'sleep hygiene' – that is, the habits we form both during the day and around bedtime that improve our ability to fall asleep and to stay asleep. Table 10.4 is adapted from the sleep hygiene guidelines offered by the American Academy of Sleep Medicine and is a chance for you to identify and plan which elements of sleep hygiene you can maintain and which you can improve.[13] If you have chronic insomnia or continue to have sleep difficulties even when practicing good sleep hygiene, see your GP to incorporate more intensive help into your self-care plan.

Mindfulness-based stress management

If you have been living under a rock for the past 20 years, you may have failed to notice the burgeoning interest in mindfulness practices. For the rest of us, mindfulness has been making its presence very much felt as it has leapt from Buddhist meditation practices into mainstream Western society, including as a therapy for chronic pain, a stress-reduction technique, an enhancer for sports performance, a practice for corporate management 'gurus'. . . and yes, as a technique for enhancing teacher wellbeing. It earns

Table 10.4 Good Sleep Hygiene

	Going Well	Needs Some Revision	Needs a Total Overhaul
I have a consistent sleep schedule; in particular, I wake up around the same time every day, even on the weekend.			
I get to bed early enough to ensure I get at least 7–8 hours of sleep each night.			
I don't go to bed until I am sleepy.			
If I am in bed but find myself worrying, I get up, carry out some quiet activity and wait for my next 'sleep wave' to come.			
I have a relaxing pre-bed wind-down routine.			
I only use my bed for sleep and sex.			
My bedroom is quiet, cool and dark to promote sleep.			
I reduce my exposure to bright light in the hour before bed.			
I get off all electronic devices half an hour before bedtime.			
I exercise regularly during the day.			
I expose myself to natural light during the day.			
I don't drink caffeinated drinks (coffee, tea, cola, etc.) after lunchtime.			
I don't drink alcohol before bedtime.			
I reduce my fluid intake at nighttime.			

its place in this discussion of self-care for teachers because we now have 20+ years of research to suggest it can genuinely help.[14]

The pioneer of mindfulness-based stress reduction, Professor Jon Kabat-Zinn from the University of Massachusetts Medical School defined mindfulness as 'paying attention in a particular way: on purpose, in the present moment and nonjudgmentally'. Definitions like this, however, are somewhat esoteric and don't really provide a sense of what mindfulness looks like in practice. I prefer the definition provided by Scott Bishop and his colleagues at the University of Toronto, who define mindfulness according to two core operational components:

> The first component involves the self-regulation of attention so that it is maintained on immediate experience, thereby allowing for increased recognition of mental events in the present moment. The second component involves adopting a particular orientation toward one's experiences in the present moment, an orientation that is characterised by curiosity, openness, and acceptance.[15]

When investigating the effectiveness of mindfulness-based interventions, researchers have incorporated a range of different mindfulness practices into their study designs. Most include the classic practice of teaching the skills of mindfulness 'meditation', but usually they also include other practices such as learning self-compassion, body scans, yoga, breathwork and visualisation.[16] Importantly, meta-analyses show that learning mindfulness can have mild to moderate beneficial effects on a range of wellbeing outcomes, including burnout, depression and anxiety. There is an important caveat: the studies on mindfulness interventions usually involve many hours of formal instruction and practice. As with most things in life, the more you put into developing mindfulness skills, the more you will get out of it. While you may find some benefits from an occasional mindfulness practise, best results are likely from more consistent application over time.

Organisational-level interventions

There is much to be said for the importance of lifestyle factors and mindfulness-based stress reduction in managing teacher stress. When these practices become a part of a person's daily routine, they are likely to significantly reduce stress and risk of burnout. An alternative approach to reducing stress in educators is to make changes at the organisational level – that is, change the environment within which teachers work. While perhaps technically not a 'self-care' strategy, it is incumbent on teachers to consider what they, with their managers, can do to reduce the stressors inherent in the workplace.

Some help is available here through a Cochrane Review. The Cochrane Library is a collection of databases containing high-quality systematic reviews that aim to evaluate scientific evidence to inform decision making across a broad range of health care domains. Recognising the high levels of stress in the teaching profession, and the health risks this creates for educators, Cochrane tasked Oxford University scholar Dr Ali Naghieh with investigating which organisational interventions in schools are most effective at improving wellbeing and reducing work-related stress.[17] Concerningly, at the time of his review, Dr Naghieh and his research team could only find four studies that met their criteria for inclusion, and those they did include had some methodological shortcomings. An obvious conclusion is that we need more research into the effects of organisational factors into teacher stress and burnout. Nonetheless, their review reported on the evidence for three types of organisational interventions. These are helpful for us to consider here as they can provide ideas for what you can seek to improve within the context of your unique work environment.

The first intervention involved changing the *task characteristics* of teachers' work. Task characteristics included changes such as establishing flexible work schedules and redesigning the work environment. The one study reporting on task characteristics found 'modest' reductions in stress levels and improvements in teachers' wellbeing. For the record, 'modest reductions' is researcher-talk for actually finding something that seems to make a helpful difference even if not earthshattering.

The second intervention they reported on related to changing the *organisational characteristics*. The studies reviewed here included training teachers to run universal programs for students aimed at improving student mental health and social-emotional functioning with the hope that a better-functioning student body would improve teacher wellbeing. Unfortunately, the two studies investigating this found that such changes had no significant effects on teacher burnout, emotional ability, job-related anxiety or job-related depression. It seems these changes may not be where you start.

The final school organisation intervention they termed a *multi-component intervention*. The 'multi-component' intervention referred to a study across 34 schools that looked at changing the way teachers could advance in their careers through getting extra pay for more responsibilities, becoming eligible for performance-based bonuses and getting mentoring support. This type of organisational change was found to moderately improve teacher retention rates.

What types of organisational changes might enhance staff wellbeing and reduce the change of burnout in your work environment? Ultimately, you and your colleagues will be the experts at identifying the most stressful components in your specific context. My hope is that you will be prompted to seriously consider what elements of your work you can change, remembering that such changes don't happen overnight but may not happen at all if staff don't participate in the process of making things happen.

Getting help

Good self-care involves getting help when you need it. We've already talked about linking up our students with appropriate help when they need it. The same principle applies for teachers. It is also the case that the same barriers to help-seeking that apply for students also apply for teachers. We worry that people will think we are weak or inadequate or crazy; we think we should be able to cope alone; we don't want to be a burden on others; we are concerned about the side effects of medicine; we convince ourselves it will get better if we can just hold on a little longer. The unfortunate reality, however, is that emotional health difficulties are the same as physical health difficulties: the longer you leave it to get help, the more difficult the task of reining back control.

The first port of call when seeking help is usually our close friends, family or colleagues. It begins with answering honestly when someone asks, 'How's work been?' Or, if they don't ask, it's about saying to a good friend, 'I'll tell you what, work has been pretty tough lately' and taking it from there. Often, breaking the ice is the hardest part. Beyond that, re-read Chapter 9 on getting help for students, but this time, come at it with the lens of getting help for yourself. Which of those help options sounds best for you? If you don't know where else to start, your local family doctor is the best port of call. Increasingly, schools and education systems are recognising the value of providing free counselling for their staff through Employee Assistance Programs (EAPs). If your school doesn't have an EAP, this might be an organisational change you can agitate to introduce.

Self-care: from theory to practice

Returning to our recipe analogy, the previous sections have outlined the 'ingredients' that you are likely to want to include in your 'meal' of good self-care. But how do you go about turning the recipe into the meal? How do you take these ideas and incorporate them into your life in such a way as to maximise your chances of effectively lowering stress and avoiding burn-out? The answer to this, I believe, is found in five interconnected principles.

Principle 1: Play the long game

Best results in implementing these self-care strategies come from seeking to incorporate them into your life over the long term. We all know the experience of commencing a well-intended diet or an exercise routine, lasting about 10 days and then reverting to our old habits. As we begin to make any important changes, we do well to picture ourselves making them for the long term and hence starting with sustainable decisions. The points that follow help contribute to the sustainability of the changes.

Principle 2: Do it with a team

Doing anything by yourself can be difficult. Making long-term life changes alone is especially difficult. We will maximise the likelihood of success to the degree that we draw a team of people around us to share the journey. The team you establish might be a simple as having a friend meet you for your end-of-the-day walks or having your family make a decision together about what time you disconnect from technology and turn off the lights at night. Your team might be a personal trainer or a dietician or a counsellor. It might be inviting a colleague to meet with you discuss some ideas about changes in your work structures to propose to the school executive.

Principle 3: Start with small achievable steps and build

If a person decides they want to run a marathon, they don't start their training by running 26 miles at their first session. Weightlifters don't start their training by lifting 150 kgs. Adopting such an approach guarantees two outcomes: failure at the first hurdle and feeling personally deflated. The best way to start making changes is by small, achievable steps. Choose one self-care strategy that appeals to you and look for small and manageable ways to implement it in your daily and weekly routine. Once you have found some rhythm with this strategy, you can build on it and add another small, achievable step, and so on.

Principle 4: Expect hiccups

Making changes doesn't happen in a linear progression. Rather, it's a matter of two steps forward, one step back. We all have better days and worse days, better weeks and worse weeks. Even with great intention, we will make mistakes and mess things up. Or sometimes, things outside of our control will put a 'spanner in the works' of our carefully developed self-care plans. None of these things, of themselves, need be a problem. More important is the way we respond in the face of these hiccups. The best response is to say, 'I knew something like this could happen. It's not what I wanted, but I'm not going to let it stop me moving forward with my plans. Today, I'll reset and get back on track as best as possible'.

Principle 5: Reward yourself

Change is hard! Even small, achievable steps require effort and persistence. Life won't give you a 'pat on the back' for your effort and persistence – you'll need to organise that yourself. Rewarding yourself is an essential strategy for staying motivated and celebrating your progress. Choose a reward that is meaningful and motivating for you. Give yourself something to look forward to. Better still, include your team in organising the reward and celebrating your progress. There is no 'finish line' in the marathon of self-care, and so we need to continually find ways to celebrate small achievements rather than waiting for some end point of perfection that will never come.

Final thoughts

We commenced this chapter with the vignette of Barney Hardin – a good teacher who had a bad few weeks. I'd like to say that Barry's story is fictitious, but sadly, it is based on an account of a real teacher and real event. Although not everyone has an incident as dramatic as Barney's, I think every teacher can relate to the way that their work wears them down to the extent that their wellbeing can be compromised.

I recently spoke with a teacher about a student in her class who was particularly challenging to manage. She was an experienced and much-loved teacher within her school, but this student had worn her down. 'I'm giving it four weeks', she told me. 'I don't need this kind of stress in my life. I've got a husband, three kids and a cat who can all see how grumpy I've become. I love my job, but if things doesn't change soon, I'm out'. This is the type of scenario that sees so many of our best educators, whether in the first year teaching or in their thirtieth year, choose to leave the profession.

Do you remember at the start of this book that I referred to some research about why people enter the teaching profession? The two primary reasons people want to work in schools are 'wanting to make a difference' and 'wanting to work with young people'. I strongly suspect that these reasons don't change as we progress in our careers. We still value these aspirations. We still see that education can make a difference for the world, and we still want to play our small part developing young people into responsible and decent adults. It's just that, when we are at the coalface, we get worn down by the workload or a lack of support or the difficulties of our most troubled students.

My sincere hope is that you can take the message of this chapter to make whatever changes you need to make in order to create a sustainable balance in your work and your life. I hope you can do that for the sake of your wellbeing but also for the sake of wellbeing of your students. This chapter won't contain all the answers you need. You'll need to talk to people, investigate more ideas, and set some manageable goals. But I hope that the chapter, and indeed this book, provides some direction to your efforts and rekindles your desire to make a difference in the lives of young people. Helping young people navigate the complexities of their emotional and behavioural health has never been more important.

In a nutshell

- Stress and burnout are genuine problems for school staff.
- How school staff function will have a flow-over effect on students – on their academic performance and on their wellbeing.

- Stress can be managed through a range of evidence-based self-care practices, including
  - Lifestyle (exercise, diet and sleep),
  - Mindfulness-based stress reduction,
  - Organisational changes, and
  - Help-seeking.
- Reading this chapter won't change your stress levels. Now, you need to form a plan and make it happen. Get to it!

Digging Deeper

1. Diliberti, M. K., Schwartz, H. L., & Grant, D. (2021). *Stress topped the reasons why public school teachers quit, even before COVID-19*. Santa Monica, CA: RAND Corporation.
2. Schaufeli, W. B., & Greenglass, E. R. (2001). Introduction to special issue on burnout and health. *Psychology and Health*, 16(5), 501–510.
3. I thank Prof. Tage Kristensen for his permission and blessing to reproduce the Copenhagen Burnout Inventory in this book. You can find his original paper describing the CBI here. Kristensen, T. S., Borritz, M., Villadsen, E., & Christensen, K. B. (2005). The Copenhagen burnout inventory: A new tool for the assessment of burnout. *Work and Stress*, 19, 192–207.
4. Madigan, D. J., & Kim, L. E. (2021). Does teacher burnout affect students? A systematic review of its association with academic achievement and student-reported outcomes. *International Journal of Educational Research*, 105, 101714.
5. Oberle, E., & Schonert-Reichl, K. A. (2016). Stress contagion in the classroom? The link between classroom teacher burnout and morning cortisol in elementary school students. *Social Science and Medicine*, 159, 30–37.
6. If you want to dig deeper on this one, check out: Bilz, L., Fischer, S. M., Hoppe-Herfurth, A.-C., & John, N. (2022). A consequential partnership: The association between teachers' well-being and students' well-being and the role of teacher support as a mediator. *Zeitschrift für Psychologie*, 230(3), 264; Harding, S., Morris, R., Gunnell, D., Ford, T., Hollingworth, W., Tilling, K., Evans, R., Bell, S., Grey, J., Brockman, R., Campbell, R., Araya, R., Murphy, S., & Kidger, J. (2019). Is teachers' mental health and wellbeing associated with students' mental health and wellbeing? *Journal of Affective Disorders*, 242, 180–187.

7   If you want to dig deeper on the relationship between physical exercise and mental health, check out: Mikkelsen, K., Stojanovska, L., Polenakovic, M., Bosevski, M., & Apostolopoulos, V. (2017). Exercise and mental health. *Maturitas*, 106, 48–56.

8   If you need convincing, I suggest you read Corbett, L., Bauman, A., Peralta, L. R., Okely, A. D., & Phongsavan, P. (2022). Characteristics and effectiveness of physical activity, nutrition and/or sleep interventions to improve the mental well-being of teachers: A scoping review. *Health Education Journal*, 81(2), 196–210; Iancu, A. E., Rusu, A., Măroiu, C., Păcurar, R., & Maricuțoiu, L. P. (2018). The effectiveness of interventions aimed at reducing teacher burnout: A meta-analysis. *Educational Psychology Review*, 30(2), 373–396; Kim, G., & Gurvitch, R. (2020). The effect of sports-based physical activity programme on teachers' relatedness, stress and exercise motivation. *Health Education Journal*, 79(6), 658–670.

9   For more on nutritional psychiatry, check out Adan, R. A. H., van der Beek, E. M., Buitelaar, J. K., Cryan, J. F., Hebebrand, J., Higgs, S., Schellekens, H., & Dickson, S. L. (2019). Nutritional psychiatry: Towards improving mental health by what you eat. *European Neuropsychopharmacology*, 29(12), 1321–1332.; Marx, W., Moseley, G., Berk, M., & Jacka, F. (2017). Nutritional psychiatry: The present state of the evidence. *Proceedings of the Nutrition Society*, 76(4), 427–436.

10 If you want to dig into the evidence for the Mediterranean diet: Lassale, C., Batty, G. D., Baghdadli, A., Jacka, F., Sánchez-Villegas, A., Kivimäki, M., & Akbaraly, T. (2019). Healthy dietary indices and risk of depressive outcomes: A systematic review and meta-analysis of observational studies. *Molecular Psychiatry*, 24(7), 965–986; Oddo, V. M., Welke, L., McLeod, A., Pezley, L., Xi, Y., Maki, P., Koenig, M. D., Kominiarek, M. A., Langenecker, S., & Tussing-Humphreys, L. (2022). Adherence to a Mediterranean diet is associated with lower depressive symptoms among U.S. adults. *Nutrients*, 14(2), 278; Ventriglio, A., Sancassiani, F., Contu, M. P., Latorre, M., Di Slavatore, M., Fornaro, M., & Bhugra, D. (2020). Mediterranean diet and its benefits on health and mental health: A literature review. *Clinical Practice and Epidemiology in Mental Health*, 16(Suppl 1), 156–164.

11 There is much debate on best descriptions of the Mediterranean diet. If you want to dig into this debate, check out Davis, C., Bryan, J., Hodgson, J., & Murphy, K. (2015). Definition of the Mediterranean diet: a literature review. *Nutrients*, 7(11), 9139–9153.

12 Consensus Conference Panel. (2015). Recommended amount of sleep for a healthy adult: A joint consensus statement of the American academy of sleep medicine and sleep research society. *Sleep*, 38(6), 843–844.

13 You can dig deeper into the American Association of Sleep Medicine's Sleep Education website here: https://sleepeducation.org/healthy-sleep/healthy-sleep-habits

14 Dig into the best summaries of the evidence for mindfulness-based interventions for teachers here: Hwang, Y.-S., Bartlett, B., Greben, M., & Hand, K. (2017). A systematic review of mindfulness interventions for in-service teachers: A tool to enhance teacher wellbeing and performance. *Teaching and Teacher Education*, 64, 26–42; von der Embse, N., Ryan, S. V., Gibbs, T., & Mankin, A. (2019). Teacher stress interventions: A systematic review. *Psychology in the Schools*, 56(8), 1328–1343; Lomas, T., Medina, J. C., Ivtzan, I., Rupprecht, S., & Eiroa-Orosa, F. J. (2017). The impact of mindfulness on the wellbeing and performance of educators: A systematic review of the empirical literature. *Teaching and Teacher Education*, 61, 132–141.

15 Bishop, S. R., Lau, M., Shapiro, S., Carlson, L., Anderson, N. D., Carmody, J., Segal, Z. V., Abbey, S., Speca, M., Velting, D., & Devins, G. (2004). Mindfulness: A proposed operational definition. *Clinical Psychology: Science and Practice*, 11(3), 230–241.

16 I use the term 'meditation' with some reluctance, as many people associate meditation with specific spiritual practices or faith traditions. Contemporary Western mindfulness mediation has become 'agnostic'. It is also worthy of consideration that mindfulness need not be considered solely a Buddhist practice, and some have sought to embrace it within other faith traditions. Dig into this further here: Stead, T. (2017). *Mindfulness and Christian spirituality: Making space for God*. Louisville, KY: Presbyterian Publishing; Niculescu, M. (2020). "Jewish mindfulness" as spiritual didactics teaching orthodox Jewish religion through mindfulness meditation. *Religions*, 11(1), 11; Thomas, J., Furber, S. W., & Grey, I. (2017). The rise of mindfulness and its resonance with the Islamic tradition. *Mental Health, Religion and Culture*, 20(10), 973–985.

17 Naghieh, A., Montgomery, P., Bonell, C. P., Thompson, M., & Aber, J. L. (2015). Organisational interventions for improving wellbeing and reducing work-related stress in teachers. *The Cochrane Database of Systematic Reviews*, 4, CD010306.

Epilogue

I am sitting in the Schools Quadrangle of the Bodleian Library at Oxford University, spending a week at an international school mental health 'round table'. Fellow attendees – stakeholders from psychology, education, social work, counselling, academia and medicine along with parents and students – have come from around the world to share and learn about best practices in the mental health management of students.

It is fitting that this gathering is held at Oxford where, for over 900 years, some of the world's keenest minds have come to learn and discover and come up with solutions to the problems of the day. It was here in the 1940s, for example, that Ernest Chain and Howard Florey refined penicillin, carried out its first test on human patients and showed the world the effectiveness of this new medicine that was to revolutionise the treatment of infections.

Decades later, our symposium is hearing of ground-breaking research that is shedding light on new solutions to old problems in students with mental health concerns. We are also hearing of dire mistakes that some have made, which we desperately hope not to see repeated. Despite our diverse backgrounds, we are discovering remarkable similarities in the challenges we face. I am reminded that what *unites* us globally is far more powerful than what makes us *different*. I am learning that the way forward rests in the effective *collaboration* of all those who work with students, each bringing their unique perspectives and skillsets. And I am increasingly convinced that, ultimately, where the 'rubber hits the road' is with those school staff who walk alongside our young people day in and day out.

The answers to the international proliferation of youth emotional distress lie in part in the ideas and discoveries of those doing robust research in universities. We need practices with demonstrated efficacy.

This is the 'head' part of the solution.

But discovering in a laboratory that penicillin is an effective treatment against infection was only helpful to the degree that it could then be rolled out to those in need. Penicillin required an 'army' of medical professionals to work with and assess their patients and give injections.

This is the 'hands' part of the solution.

Similarly, we need educators who are trained and equipped to bring evidence-based ideas into their interactions with students, particularly those students with emotional and behavioural disorders. School staff are the interface between brilliant ideas and the young people we serve.

But it takes more than just good ideas and an army of implementers. Medical practitioners acknowledge the importance of, and work hard to develop, sound skills in the so-called 'bedside manner'. Interestingly, injected penicillin will go about its work attacking infection regardless of the quality of the medical practitioner's bedside manner.

The same can't be said for educators rolling out interventions with students.

As I re-read the final manuscript of this book, I have been surprised at the number of times I have referred to the importance of having *compassion* for our students. Compassion is not an idea that gets a lot of headlines in the theory of education or psychology. But it is important.

This is the 'heart' part of the solution.

Without the heart of compassion, the ideas of the head and the implementation of our hands are meaningless.

And so, out we must venture . . . with head, hands and heart.

Index

academic performance; and mental health 11
Adams, Zachary 45
anxiety 38–41; panic attacks 41; selective mutism 40–41; separation anxiety 39; social anxiety disorder 40; specific phobia 39–40
arousal symptoms 46
assessing student risk 92–93
attention deficit hyperactivity disorder (ADHD) 52–57; medication 55–57
avoidance symptoms 46

behavioural clues 37
bell curve 28
Berg, Insoo Kim 109
bipolar disorder 68–70; bipolar 1 vs. bipolar 2 69
Bishop, Scott 167–168
borderline personality disorder 70–71
Brave Program 150
burnout 155–158; definition 155

Child and Adolescent Mental Health and Educational Outcome Study 9
Chilled Out 150
classroom approaches 97–115; engaging learning environment 101–102; modified learning environment 106–108; relational learning environment 103–104; safe learning environment 104–106
classroom behaviour 10; management 29–30
classroom modifications for students with emotional and behavioural disorders *see* classroom approaches
cognitive behavioural therapy 57
Collaborative and Proactive Solutions (CPS) 29, 86–87, 111–114
comorbidity 61
conduct disorder *see* externalising disorders
CoolKids Online 150
Copenhagen Burnout Inventory (CBI) 156–159; client-related burnout 157; personal burnout 156; scoring and interpreting 158–159; work-related burnout 156
cosmetic psychodermatology 74–75
Costello, Jane 26
cultural considerations in mental health 149

depression 41–44; major depressive disorder 42–43; prevalence 43; risk factors 43–44
de Shazer, Steve 109
The Diagnostic and Statistical Manual of Mental Disorders 31–32

Index

diet *see* self-care
disruptive behaviour disorders 51
dissociative symptoms 46
drug and alcohol use 165
duration of concerns 30
Duration of Untreated Illness (DUI) 27
duty of care 22–26

early psychosis 72
eating disorders 66–68; anorexia nervosa 66–67; avoidant/restrictive food intake disorder 67; binge-eating disorder 67; bulimia nervosa 67
emotions clues 38
empathy step 86–89
Employee Assistance Programs (EAPs) 170
externalising disorders 32, 51–63; attention deficit hyperactivity disorder (ADHD) 52–57; classroom management 58–60; conduct disorder 57–58; oppositional defiant disorder 57

Freud, Sigmund 108

Gillies, Donna 119
Greene, Ross 29, 86–87, 111
Greenglass, Esther 156

Health Commission's National Mental Health and Wellbeing Strategy 14–15
help for students with emotional and behavioural disorders 135–146; community-based mental health clinics 143–144; dial emergency 146; general practitioners (GPs) 142–143; hospital emergency departments 144–145; medication 137–139; online interventions 150; when students/parents refuse help 146–148; talking therapies 139–140; telehealth 149–150; telephone help lines 144; whose job is it? 135–136

Incredible Years Teacher Management Program 60
information sharing 23–26; duty of care 25; student age 25–26; student consent 24
internalising disorders 32
International Statistical Classification of Diseases and Related Health Problems (ICD) 31–32
intrusive symptoms 45

Jorm, Anthony 16

Kabat-Zinn, Jon 167
Kelly, Claire 16
Kim, Lisa 161
Kitchener, Betty 16

LGBTQI students 67, 104, 149

Madigan, Daniel 161
mania 68–69
medical model 108
medication *see* help for students with emotional and behavioural disorders
Mediterranean diet 164–165
mental health crisis 13
mental health first aid 15–16
Mental Health Literacy 15–16
Mental Health of Children and Adolescents: Report on the second Australian Child and Adolescent Survey of Mental Health and Wellbeing 9, 26
mindfulness-based stress management *see* self-care
Moodgym 150

Naghieh, Ali 169
NAPLAN *see* National Assessment Program - Numeracy and Literacy
National Assessment Program – Numeracy and Literacy (NAPLAN) 9
National Children's Mental Health and Wellbeing Strategy 14–15

negative mood 46
nutritional psychiatry 164

Oberle, Eva 161
obsessive compulsive disorders 73–75; body dysmorphia 74–75; obsessive compulsive disorder (OCD) 73–74
online interventions *see* help for students with emotional and behavioural disorders
oppositional defiant disorder *see* externalising disorders

panic attacks *see* anxiety
parent management training 57
pathways to care 135
physical and body clues 37
physical exercise *see* self-care
privacy 23–26
prodromal *see* early psychosis
psychiatrisation 46–47
psychotic illness 71–72; prevalence 72; schizophrenia 72

raising concerns with students 85–89
Rand Corporation 155
refugee students 104
return to school plan *see* suicidal students

Saunders, Benjamin 45
Schaufeli, Wilmar 156
schizophrenia *see* psychotic illness
Schneider, Sophie 74–75
Schonert-Reichl, Kimberley 161
selective mutism *see* anxiety
self-care 159–173; and academic performance 161; definition 159–160; diet 164–165; getting help 170; lifestyle factors 162–166 (diet 164–165; mindfulness-based stress management 166–168; physical exercise 163–164; sleep 165–167);

organisational-level interventions 168–170; and student wellbeing 161; from theory to practice 170–172
self-harm 118–123; assessing 122–123; attitude to 120–121; reasons 119; responding to 123; types 119–120
separation anxiety *see* anxiety
sleep *see* self-care
social anxiety disorder *see* anxiety
solution focused therapy 109
specific phobia *see* anxiety
standardised mortality ratio (SMR) 67–68
strengths-based approaches 108–110
stress contagion theory 161
substance use disorders 75–77
suicidal students 124–127; assessment 125–126, 128; prevalence 124; responding to 127; return to school plan 129; school policy 128

teacher stress 11, 154–155
teacher-student relationship 83–85
Teaching and Learning International Study (TALIS) 11–12, 154–155
telehealth *see* help for students with emotional and behavioural disorders
therapy *see* help for students with emotional and behavioural disorders
thinking clues 37
trauma 44–46; acute stress disorder 44–45; adjustment disorder 44–45; post-traumatic stress disorder (PTSD) 44; prevalence 45; symptoms 45–46
treatment; students not receiving 26–27
Twenge, Jean 13

upstream vs downstream staff 22

Van Meter, Anna 124

wellbeing 26

For Product Safety Concerns and Information please contact our EU representative GPSR@taylorandfrancis.com
Taylor & Francis Verlag GmbH, Kaufingerstraße 24, 80331 München, Germany

www.ingramcontent.com/pod-product-compliance
Lightning Source LLC
Chambersburg PA
CBHW070309230426
43664CB00015B/2693